# Praise for *Jesus Prom*

"If you want a book making the gospel message accessible to young and old and to people who've had difficulty finding their way in, you've found it."

—Bob Goff, author of *Love Does*, from the foreword

"This is brilliant writing. An economy of words that cut right to the heart, keep you turning pages, and ignite within a passion to live 'Jesus Prom' style. I loved this book."

—Ken Davis, author of *Fully Alive*

"I love the message of *Jesus Prom* because it so faithfully captures the message of Jesus. Jon Weece's writing is compassionate and convicting as he gives us an incredible picture of what love looks like in action. *Jesus Prom* will move you, and your church, to find joy in authentically representing Jesus!"

—Jud Wilhite, author of *Pursued*, senior pastor of Central Christian Church

"Heartwarming stories of love that will help you dance with Jesus. Take as a tonic for a weary soul."

—Robert Coleman, author of *The Master Plan of Evangelism*

# JESUS PROM

*For Brewster and those who dance with him*

# Contents

# foreword

## BY BOB GOFF

I bought a building once and was going to turn it into dozens of offices. It was a beautiful turn-of-the-century Victorian with many rooms, each with its own fireplace. Some had private staircases leading to them. This beautiful building even had a huge walk-in safe. I found out Wyatt Earp, the famous lawman and gambler, used to own this place and worked there. That would explain the safe.

When we were in the middle of renovations, we realized something we hadn't given any thought to originally. There was no way for people with disabilities to get into the building. The place had plenty of steps. There were hundreds in the house. It was practically made of them. But what the building needed were more ramps. All the steps in the world won't help some people get into places that aren't accessible to them. Ironically, it's the steps that keep these people out rather than making it easier for them to get in.

Certainly, the people who designed the building weren't trying to keep anyone out. Wyatt Earp probably wasn't.

The guy who owned the building before me wasn't trying to keep people out either. As we looked a little closer at the building, the steps had almost become one of its defining characteristics. We knew we needed to change that. So we put in ramps where there once were stairs. We wanted people who'd had trouble with steps to still get in. Jon wants the same thing for all of us.

This is a book about ramps. It's stories about hundreds of ways for people to get to Jesus. If you want a book with a bunch of steps in it, this isn't the one for you. If you want a book making the gospel message accessible to young and old and to people who've had difficulty finding their way in, you've found it. This isn't a book full of facts and information; it's a book full of stories. And Jon is one of the best storytellers I've heard. He tells beautiful stories about hope and grace and acceptance and forgiveness. He talks about the power of being present in people's lives and the beauty of living a life of availability and inconvenience. This is a book about God's tremendous love and accessibility to everybody—even if they don't roll the way you roll.

One of the other things I like about Jon is that he doesn't make everything about him. He's a guy who doesn't need spotlights. Bright lights never do. He avoids them the way I avoid dentists. Humble guys with a fearsome love for God will still draw people in. People come from all around to hear Jon. I've been to his church. It's huge. It could be its own small country if they made a flag. But Jon doesn't care about any of that. If you asked him how many people show up on a Sunday, he'd probably round it down to the one person standing in front of him. That's because Jon sees things guys like me overlook. He only sees the person right in front of him.

He knows the power of inconvenient love and relentless pursuit. He also knows that if we keep making everything about us, it'll never be about Jesus. So Jon doesn't even try to make it about him. He just tells us in these pages what he's seen God doing and lets us connect the dots about why God's love for humanity is that big. Jon's organized his thoughts around a couple of key words—it's a beautiful idea. It's not a book about grammar though; it's a book about engagement, inclusion, and living a life of inexplicable love.

Jon and I have sat together at the end of an inlet in Canada and talked about life and love and Jesus. Just like I did when I read this book, I found myself belly laughing at Jon's stories in one moment, then quietly nodding my head in agreement in another.

One afternoon while Jon was with me, he took a kayak out for a paddle. I hadn't given him directions about kayaking around the area and he hadn't asked for any. He told me about his trip later. Jon said he had been paddling for a while and went through a small passage that had some really large rocks on each side. He said at one point the paddling got a little more difficult, but he didn't give it much thought and just paddled harder.

What Jon still has no idea about is that he had just paddled through some of the most dangerous rapids in all of British Columbia. No one goes through those rapids when they're running. I've been up the inlet for twenty years and I haven't done it. Two-hundred-foot yachts with professional captains who have tried to navigate these waters have ended up on the rocks.

Jon had hit the rapids during the few moments in the day when the tidal waters were changing directions. I think Jon's done the same thing with this book. He'd tell you he just stumbled upon some of these ideas, but that wouldn't be true. This is a book from a humble guy who sees the tide changing directions in our faith communities and he's invited us to navigate those changes together. Jon draws deeply on the power of love and the examples Jesus and His friends left us to be our guides.

Let me introduce you to my friend Jon. Get ready to put your paddles in the water. You're in for a treat.

# start (v.) here (adv.)

I nearly flunked English grammar. Ask Mrs. Harding, my seventh-grade grammar teacher, and she'll validate that. But this much I know: The word *Christian* is a noun. A Christian is a person who follows Jesus. *Follow* is a verb. And I've learned over the years that nouns need verbs.

Jesus loved verbs. Verbs like *love, come, rest, learn, hear, die, give,* and *go.* So wouldn't it make sense that the people who claim to follow Jesus would love the same verbs Jesus loved?

Somewhere along the way someone tried to make the word *Christian* an adjective. So now people speak of Christian (adj.) books and Christian (adj.) music and Christian (adj.) T-shirts and Christian (adj.) schools. When people use the word *Christian* as an adjective, instead of a noun that loves verbs, it loses its meaning. Maybe this explains why so many churches have lost their meaning too.

If a Christian is a person (singular) who follows Jesus, then the church is made of people (plural) who follow Jesus. And like a Christian, the church is a noun too—a noun designed to love verbs. Specifically, it is a noun that should love the same verbs Jesus loved because the church is a picture of Jesus.

I don't mean this as an indictment, but it seems as though some of us have lost our verbs.

When we lose our verbs, we become what the world claims we are: hypocrites. A hypocrite is nothing more than a noun without a verb. Lovers who don't love . . . Givers who don't give . . . Followers who don't follow . . .

We need fewer adjectives and more verbs. Have you noticed the adjectives we put in front of the noun *Christian*?

"She's such a loving Christian."

"He's such a giving Christian."

*Loving. Giving.*

Is there any other kind of Christian? Can a Christian be a Christian without loving and giving? If a Christian doesn't love or give, is that person really a Christian? Maybe a better way to ask the question is: Can a Christian be unloving or not a giving person?

Or have you noticed the adjectives we put in front of the noun *church*?

> *Baptist* church
> *Lutheran* church

*Traditional* church
*Contemporary* church
*Black* church
*White* church

The word appearing before the word *church* in the New Testament more than any other word is the word *the*.

*The* church.

*The* church at Philippi . . . *The* church at Thessalonica . . . *The* church at Ephesus . . .

I like the word Jesus put in front of the word *church*. Jesus told Peter, "The gates of hell will not prevail against *My* church" (Matt. 16:18, author's paraphrase, emphasis added).

I really like that.

*His* church.

In the same way that the church belongs to Jesus, I belong to Jesus. And you belong to Jesus.

*We* belong to Jesus.

He is *the* leader.

We follow (v.) Him.

When we follow Jesus, we don't need adjectives to describe us.

I am a Christian. We are the church. Period.

When we follow Jesus, we will love the way Jesus loves. When we follow Jesus, we will give the way Jesus gives. It's not the adjective before the noun that matters. It's the verb after the noun we need to pay attention to.

In this book I want to paint a simple picture of a simple person (a Christian) and simple people (the church) who love the verbs Jesus loved. If we love the verbs Jesus loved, I'm convinced we will love the people He loves. That's when life gets fun! And a fun verb to start with is the verb *jump*.

When I was in the fourth grade, I was invited to a birthday party at Chris's house. I was excited because it was the first birthday party I had been to where girls had also been invited. Specifically, Sarah Grossnickle had been invited.

Her last name is a bit unfortunate. But she was stunning, and she had braces. I don't know why I was so enamored with braces as a kid, but I was. Maybe the thought of having rubber bands in my mouth seemed so handy to me. Or maybe it was the thought of having a girl in my class with straight teeth someday.

I just know I was head over heels in love with Sarah Grossnickle. I sent her several notes in class with a box to check. *Yes. No. Maybe.* On two separate occasions she checked the box that said *Maybe*, but I was about to give her a reason to check the box that said *Yes*.

Everyone in my class was standing on the deck in Chris's

backyard. His parents were putting in a pool and had dug a huge hole, and there was a large pile of dirt about ten feet from the deck. So as ten-year-old boys do, a dare was thrown out.

"Who wants to play Follow the Leader?"

I was eating a box of Junior Mints when I accepted the dare. (It was easily my third or fourth box.) I wanted to set the bar high—so high no one would be able to follow me. So I marked off my steps. The drumroll began. And Sarah smiled at me, which was all the motivation I needed.

I could actually hear the song "You're the Inspiration" by Chicago playing in my mind as I took off running. With speed and momentum I planted my right foot on the railing of the deck to jump. However, the railing gave way. Instead of going up, I went straight down.

Fortunately for me, a nail caught the edge of my pants and slowed me down. Unfortunately for me, that nail ripped my pants completely off and I went sailing headfirst into a pile of bricks stacked neatly below the deck.

When I came to, I was headed for the emergency room. I was sitting in my Fruit of the Looms in the back of a Cadillac with leather interior. And let's just say the ol' Junior Mints were not agreeing with me. The only tactful way for me to put this is to say I "relinquished ownership" of the Junior Mints, and no product on the market could have cleaned up the mess I created in the backseat of that luxury automobile.

No one followed me over the railing that day. I was the only one who jumped.

Somewhere between that deck and the desk where I'm sitting right now, I lost the courage to take risks. Some might blame it on maturity. Others might point the finger at intelligence. But I think the more birthdays we have, the fewer verbs we have. Our verb vocabulary shrinks with time.

Somewhere along the way, I went to college, got married, had two kids, got a grown-up job, bought a house, started a 401(k), and somehow ended up driving a minivan. (I'm still not sure how that one happened.)

In the midst of the *have to*, it's easy to lose sight of the *get to*.

I *get to* follow Jesus.

He is *the* leader. He is *my* leader. He is *your* leader. He is *our* leader.

We get to follow Jesus. What a privilege! And when we follow Jesus, He doesn't lead us to places as often as He leads us to people. That's why there is nothing safe about following Jesus. Following Jesus is simple, but it's not safe.

My prayer for you is simple but not safe. So simple it's a single word. It's a verb.

*Jump.*

It's a verb that is looking for a noun.

I think *you* are the missing noun. Insert your name here: _____ jumped today.

It may seem safe to stand on the deck with everyone else. But standing on the deck is not safe. It's boring. So go for it.

Jump.

Set down whatever you are holding, or whatever has hold of you.

And jump.

Helen Keller said, "Life is either a daring adventure or nothing."

Decide today that you are going to follow *the* leader. Decide today that you are going to be on a first-name basis with the emergency room staff in a hospital near you. Decide today that you are going to trade *what is* for *what could be*.

I dare you to jump.

# PART ONE

# *Christian*—the person (n.) who loves (v.) people

ONE

# love (v.)

It was a Saturday morning. When I lived in Haiti, that's when I went to the open-air market to buy my food for the week. I was standing in the middle of the street holding a bag filled with oranges, rice, and beans. And that was when I saw him. It was as though a page had been torn out of a *National Geographic* magazine, then framed for me to stare at.

His legs were disproportionate in size to the rest of his body, bent at angles unfamiliar to a healthy torso. His head was bowed in shame, but I could tell he was blind because his eyes never really fixed on any particular object. Rather, they danced from side to side and followed the noises around him. He was barely clothed, and his body was caked with dust and dirt. His hair was matted down from sweat, and flies took up residence on his skin.

His hands were outstretched. He was holding a small bowl. He was begging.

I watched as one person after another passed by him . . .

ignored him . . . pretended he didn't exist. Then he pulled a small board from his bag and placed it in the sewage that ran beside the road. Blocking its flow, he did something I wish I could scrub from my memory. He placed his hands in the raw sewage and began to sift and search as if looking for something of value. While living in Haiti, I had watched a woman drink from a mud puddle and had caught two men eating garbage, but this was a new low.

My heart broke and scattered into pieces I will not recover this side of heaven.

I watched as he pulled out an old battery. He cleaned it off as if it were a rare artifact missing from a prestigious museum. He slid it under his leg like someone might come looking for it.

With tears streaming down my cheeks, I knelt down in front of him and took his dirty hands, placed them on my face, and in Kreyol said, "My name is Jon, and I want to be your friend."

That's all I could get out. I couldn't talk, but he could.

"Thank you," he whispered.

As much as he needed me, I needed him. Love is never independent. Love is always dependent. Someone always gives. Someone always receives.

"My parents broke my legs when I was a baby so that I could beg and bring in money for our family," he said.

I filled his empty bag with my bagful of food. I filled his pocket with my pocketful of money. Love empties itself, because love emptied Himself.

Jesus asked a blind man named Bartimaeus, "What do you want Me to do for you?"

That's always the question love asks: *What can I do for you?*

―――――――

I have a friend named Donnie. When Donnie was six years old, he watched his dad beat up his mom. The trauma of that episode locked Donnie into a permanent state of childlikeness. Though he is fifty-two years of age today, Donnie thinks and acts and communicates like a six-year-old. Donnie loves me, and I love Donnie. He has taught me a lot about love.

Donnie washed dishes at a local restaurant for two decades. Each Friday he would cash his paycheck, and each Saturday he would ride his bike from one garage sale to the next buying albums and paper novels and costume jewelry. Donnie has a Christmas gift list with 385 people on it. Donnie loves people, and people love Donnie—so much so that he spends his entire year Christmas shopping for all the people he loves.

One of my prized possessions is a ring that looks as if it came from a gumball machine. Maybe it did. I don't really care *where* it came from because I know *who* it came from. I know it came from Donnie. I know it came from Donnie's heart.

Donnie understands Christmas better than most people do. Donnie couldn't tell you *where* Jesus came from. But Donnie does know *who* sent Jesus. And Donnie knows *why* the Father sent Jesus: love.

Donnie doesn't know a stranger. When he meets people for the first time, he hugs them. And he doesn't let go! When Donnie hugs people, he holds on! And it doesn't matter who you are; once Donnie learns your name, your name finds its way onto his Christmas list. From the mayor of our city to the homeless men in Phoenix Park, Donnie knows a lot of people by name.

Donnie looks a lot like love.

Love holds on.

Love gives.

Love knows.

Donnie is on a fixed income. But God isn't. He never runs out of anything.

The Bible teaches that God *is* love, which means He never runs out of it. No matter how great the demand for love is, God is never in short supply. And what I love about God is He doesn't love things the way people love things. God loves people.

More specifically, God loves you.

He wants to hold you, give to you, and know you. And He wants you to do the same for others. John wrote, "Whoever does not love does not know God, because God is love" (1 John 4:8). John referred to himself as "the disciple whom Jesus loved" (John 21:20).

How do you refer to yourself?

If you don't feel loved, it's not because you aren't loved.

One of the ways to get love is to give love.

Most Tuesdays I stand on a corner in the downtown district of my hometown with a sign that says Free Hugs. I've done it for more than a decade now. One man looked at my sign for a while, shrugged his shoulders in a disappointed tone, and said, "I thought it said Free Hogs!" Only in Kentucky would someone be sad that I wasn't giving away free farm animals!

My favorite street corner is across the street from the courthouse. As part of sentencing, a local judge sends those he convicts to me. And as part of their punishment, they have to hug me. I get a lot of side-hugs from the men.

One lady rode up on a bike not too long ago and said, "What does your sign say?" She couldn't read. So I told her what it said. She cocked her head to the side and took another drag from the cigarette she was smoking. Then she squinted and said, "Are you for real?"

"Come a little closer and find out," I said.

So she got off her bike, and I went in for the kill. When I tried to pull away from her, she pulled me in tighter. She buried her head in my chest and said, "Nobody's hugged me in a long time."

When nobody hugs you, you begin to feel like a nobody.

Nobody is a nobody to God. Everybody is a somebody to God.

One of the ways we experience His love for us is by giving His love to others. And there's no way to give love away without getting closer. God doesn't try to love us at a distance. God came down, and love came with Him. And God doesn't stiff-arm anyone who needs to be loved.

God doesn't give side-hugs.

One weekend after preaching, I went into the bathroom at one of our campuses. As I was standing there, I felt two arms wrap themselves around me from behind. Someone was hugging me while I was going to the bathroom.

A man is defenseless in that position. And speechless. There is an unwritten code of conduct in a men's bathroom. You look straight ahead, and you don't talk to the man next to you. You can talk once you get to the sink or on your way out the door, but not at the toilet. It's all business there. For women, a trip to the bathroom is a social function. Women share fashion tips and parenting ideas in the bathroom. (Or so I've heard.)

Someone wanted to share a hug with me . . . in the bathroom . . . from behind. Then I heard the voice.

"I love you, Jon."

As if the hug from behind wasn't awkward enough, now I had a grown man telling me he loved me. Every other grown man in the bathroom laughed out loud—though not in a mean way.

"I love you too, Tim," I said.

Tim is one of the many people in our church with special needs. Every Sunday our conversation is the same. After he tells me he loves me and after I tell him I love him, Tim says, "You look nice today."

"You look nice too," I say back.

Tim then says, "You're my preacher."

And I say, "And you're my friend."

Then he smiles from ear to ear and gives me a huge hug. But this time, the hug came first.

Is there a sequence to love? The Bible says there is: "We love because he first loved us" (1 John 4:19). God loves us. And because of His love for us, we are then able to love Him and others in return.

God initiates. We reciprocate. That's the sequence.

I believe the answer to all the world's problems is love. Some have called me naïve for believing that, but I've been called worse things. My problem is, I can't think of a problem that can't be solved by love.

I can't think of a problem Love can't solve.

Bartimaeus was blind. Most people would say blindness is a physical problem. Or, blindness is a medical problem.

I agree.

But like all other problems, blindness creates other problems too. No problem is an island to itself. When Bartimaeus asked Jesus for help, the crowd told him to be quiet. That's a problem. What gave the crowd the right to tell a man in need to be quiet? If Jesus could solve Bartimaeus's problem, why didn't the crowd want Bartimaeus to get the help he needed? The selfishness of the crowd was a bigger problem than the blindness of Bartimaeus.

Selfishness is the opposite of love. Love is selfless.

My problem is, I'm not. I'm not selfless. I'm selfish. I can say it's *my* problem, but I know how selfishness works. My selfishness doesn't just affect me. My selfishness affects others. It can't be contained. Selfishness is toxic to my heart. If I try to bury it, if I try to hide it, it always leaks—and it always poisons my relationships.

My selfishness hurts others, and it hurts me. But when I am selfless, it helps others and it helps me.

I can never love people too much. My wife. My kids. My friends. My coworkers. I haven't met a person who needs to be loved less. I have met people who need to be loved differently. What some people receive as love, and perceive to be love, is not love. But what echoes in the chambers of my heart is, "Love never fails" (1 Cor. 13:8).

Love *never* fails?

Ever.

That's why Jesus said, "Love your enemies" (Matt. 5:44). When we love our enemies, they become our friends. Just like love, everyone needs more friends.

I had a woman tell me one time, "You preach too much about love." I didn't know that was possible. So I thanked her for letting me know. But she wasn't done!

"You need to preach about deeper things," she said in a demanding tone. I didn't know there was anything deeper than God's love. I've been exploring God's love for years, and I've yet to get to the bottom of it.

My friend Gary started mentoring an at-risk boy in a local elementary school. The first time Gary met the boy, the boy said, "I want to stab you."

"I want to love you," Gary said.

No one had probably ever said that to that boy.

Years later, they were walking down a hallway together and the boy said, "I want to hold your hand."

From "I want to stab you" to "I want to hold your hand." From knife-in-hand to hand-in-hand.

Love never fails. Ever.

Jesus didn't listen to the crowd. Jesus listened to Bartimaeus. Jesus helped Bartimaeus because Jesus loved Bartimaeus, and He cared for Bartimaeus by asking Bartimaeus what he needed.

Love asks. Love never assumes. One of the best questions we can ask people is, how can I love you? Too often we assume we know how people need to be loved or want to be loved.

One day, I picked up a hitchhiker who was barefoot. After buying him some shoes, I told him he could borrow my car anytime he needed it. He laughed. "I like walking," he said.

I had assumed he needed a car.

"But I do need to see a doctor," he added. I couldn't tell from looking, but his back hurt. So I called a friend of mine who is a doctor, and he was able to help him.

Don't assume. Ask.

I was driving down one of the busiest roads in Lexington when I saw an older woman seated on a bench near a bus stop. Because it was raining and because I had an appointment to make, I didn't stop. As I drove past her, the Spirit reminded me that Jesus put His life on hold to give life to people like me. So I turned around, drove back to the bus stop, and got out of my car. As I walked toward her, she got a scared look on her face and put her foot up as if I was going to tackle her.

Seeing she was terrified, I gently said, "Can I give you a ride somewhere?"

"No thanks," she said.

So I asked, "What can I do for you?"

"I'm hungry and I need to get my prescriptions filled," she said as she looked down through fogged-up glasses. Across the street were a pharmacy and a fast-food restaurant. It's not always that easy. But that day it was easy. She was easy to love, even if she didn't receive love with ease.

The more I love people, the more I fall in love with God. The more I fall in love with God, the more I love people.

Bartimaeus got more than his sight from Jesus. Bartimaeus got a friend in Jesus. Bartimaeus learned what love looks like. Bartimaeus stared Love in the face.

What a face to see . . .

———————

Several years after watching the Haitian man pull the battery and pennies from a sewer, I saw him again. I was cleaning up a beach with some of our students when I heard a familiar sound in the distance. As the noise drew closer, a young man walked around the corner with a rope tied to his waist. He was pulling a makeshift wheelchair. Seated in the wheelchair was the man I had encountered on the side of the road years earlier.

He had taken a piece of PVC pipe and fashioned a flute from it, and he was playing the children's song "Jesus Loves Me." I set my shovel down.

I gave some money to the young man who was leading him, and he whispered something to the old man. I knelt down beside his chair, and he smiled and said to me, "Can I pray for you?"

"Please do," I eagerly said.

He removed his straw hat, raised his eyes to heaven, and said, "Father, help my brother to see You the way that I see You."

Sometimes we don't need our sight to see Jesus. Sometimes we see Jesus in the faces of those who have been loved by Him and those who love like Him.

# TWO

# be (v.)

One evening after work, I turned onto our street. As I was driving toward the cul-de-sac where our house sits, I saw a little boy—maybe five years of age—throw open his front door and burst out. It was the dead of winter, and all he was wearing were his Superman Underoos and a bath-towel-turned-cape tied around his neck. He ran parallel to me on the sidewalk, and as I glanced out the passenger-side window, he locked eyes with me and smiled. (Did I mention that his mom was chasing him with a wooden spoon yelling, "Stop! Stop!"?)

It was like a Norman Rockwell painting set in motion.

The grin on his face said, *Free at last! Free at last! Thank God Almighty I'm free at last!*

Later in the spring I saw him buried in a mud puddle up to his neck. My kind of boy! A few weeks later I watched him jump his bike off a massive pile of dirt, still wearing nothing but his Underoos, an oversize motorcycle helmet, and a pair of winter gloves. It was like watching Evel Knievel jump the fountains at Caesar's Palace again.

"I have to meet this kid!" I told my wife, Allison.

The very next night, I was at the neighborhood park with my two children when I saw him. He was swinging on the swings as high as they could possibly carry him. And as I walked toward him, he jumped at the height of the upswing—arms flailing, legs kicking. All I heard was "Geronimo!" He hit the ground like a stuntman, rolled through the mulch, and jumped to his feet.

"Son, what is your name?" I asked.

He put his hands on his hips and with a superhero's pose, he said, "My name is Christian."

I nodded my head and said, "Oh, how fitting."

At the heart of being a Christian is being a child. As adults we've become a culture of *human doings,* when we were designed to live as *human beings.* And when we deny our design, we run the risk of destroying our design. The verb *to be* is a verb that flows from the blueprints of our Designer.

God was.

God is.

And God will always . . . *be.*

And God has invited you to be His child.

"See what great love the Father has lavished on us, that we should be [v.] called children of God. And that is what we are!" (1 John 3:1).

When my wife, Allison, was twenty-eight weeks pregnant with our first child, she called me to let me know that her feet were swollen. Water retention is not an uncommon occurrence in pregnancy. But just to be safe, she stopped at a drugstore to check her blood pressure. Sure enough, the numbers were sky-high. Allison called our doctor, and he invited her to come in for a quick checkup. I met her at the hospital thinking it would be a routine visit.

I could tell from the look on the doctor's face that something wasn't right. After running a few tests, he informed us that Allison would need to be on bed rest for the duration of her pregnancy. That curveball hit us from left field. Twelve weeks is a long time to be in bed, and we were not expecting that news.

After more tests that day, we learned Allison would need to stay in the hospital for her bed rest. That was an even bigger blow. And less than an hour later, the doctor sat down on the edge of Allison's bed, and I could see the sadness in his body language.

"I hate to tell you this, but it looks like you are going to deliver your baby within the night," he said.

As those words rolled out of his mouth, a team of nurses

came in the room and started hooking my wife up to all kinds of machines. It happened so fast. And the tears came just as quickly for us. My prayers went from very generic prayers of, "God, help us deal with this," to very desperate and lonely cries of, "God, I beg of You . . . please work a miracle on behalf of my wife and little girl."

I wasn't questioning God. I wasn't asking, "Why me? Why my wife? Why my firstborn child?" I've lived in this fragile and fallen world long enough to know this truth: God is good even when life isn't good to me.

By morning Allison's physical condition had worsened, and doctors feared we would lose her if we didn't deliver the life inside of her. I was tired of being tired. I was scared and worried, but strangely I was excited too. I was going to meet my daughter. I was going to be a dad. That doesn't happen every day!

Fifteen minutes later, Ava Joy was born—all two pounds of her—three months early.

At least ten doctors discussed with Allison and me all the potential complications Ava could face in life—hearing loss, blindness, and a litany of other developmental challenges. Honestly, the list was longer than I could have imagined. But at the time, that list didn't matter to me. I was a dad. And dads don't care what their children can or can't do. We love them! And the reason I loved Ava was because she was mine. I helped make her. Part of me was in her.

In the middle of the night, when no one else was around,

I stared into the little glass tube where my little girl was fighting for her life. And it hit me—God has heard all the reports on me. And in spite of how grave they are, in spite of my spiritual prematurity, He loves me. Because in the purest, truest sense of the word, God is a dad.

And part of Him is in me. And part of Him is in you.

We are His children, and He loves us as we are.

I stood over Ava's incubator and wanted what was best for her. Whatever the cost, whatever the procedure, I pleaded with the doctors to do what they could to help her live.

When I read the Bible, it is like a love letter from a lovesick dad to His homesick children. And in it He says, "Whatever the cost, whatever the procedure—even if it means giving My life for yours—I will do it, I will pay it, I will go through it for you so you can live!"

I watched medical professionals cut my daughter, poke her, prod her, and put her through the proverbial medical ringer. And through all of it, I didn't want her to go through it alone. So I would sit by her bed. I would stand by her bed. I would eat and sleep by her bed. I wanted her to hear and know my voice.

When I read the Bible, I hear the voice of my Father say, "I will never fail you. I will never abandon you" (Heb. 13:5 NLT).

I stood over Ava's incubator so proudly. I sang, "Jesus loves you, this I know, for the Bible tells me so." And when I got to the part in the song that says, "Little ones to Him belong; they are weak, but He is strong," I would cry. My daughter was so small I could fit my wedding band over her thigh.

I still can't sing that song without crying because of Zephaniah's words: "The LORD your God is with you, he is mighty to save. He will take great delight in you, he will quiet you with his love, he will rejoice over you with singing" (Zeph. 3:17).

You have a Dad who sings over you. He's so proud of you. The Bible teaches that He has your name written on the palm of His hand—the same hand that took a nail for you. He didn't go through that pain so you could spend your entire life questioning whether or not He really loves you. He *really* loves you.

And before you can be His follower, you have to be His child.

That was a challenge for a man named Nicodemus.

Nicodemus was having one of those nights. Tossing and turning, counting sheep, and drinking warm glasses of milk weren't helping him. Tempur-Pedic couldn't solve his restlessness. So he got up, slipped on his coat and hat, and made his way across town to a house where Jesus was staying.

I don't know if he went to be with Jesus at night because he was afraid of being seen with Jesus. I don't know if he went to be with Jesus at night because he was experiencing a dark night of the soul.

What I do know is Nicodemus had clout dripping off him. Nicodemus was an insider—a man who ran in the fast lane of the rich and famous. The Talmud says he was one of the richest men in Jerusalem. He was highly educated, highly successful, and highly respected. And I would bet that it was his birth certificate that afforded him the opportunity to become part of an even more elite crowd known as the Pharisees.

Scholars tell us there were about six thousand Pharisees in Jesus' day. They were sworn to be strict observers of the law, but they had twisted the good nature of God's law and made it burdensome for all who were subjected to it.

Not only was Nicodemus a member of the Pharisee ranks, but he was also a member of the Sanhedrin—seventy of the sharpest Jewish minds who had been chosen to rule over the entire Jewish nation. They were powerful, they were looked up to, and they were also extremely prideful.

Nicodemus went to Jesus that night as a leader and a scholar, but mostly as a man whose restless heart wouldn't let his mind go to sleep. He went knocking that night, titles and résumé in hand, impressive credentials unlike any in his day—but Jesus wouldn't open the door until He had stripped Nicodemus of the accolades the world had given him.

Jesus told him, "You must be born again" (John 3:7). He may not have cared about Nicodemus's credentials, but He did care about Nicodemus.

We are born into a world that repeatedly asks us, "What do you want to be when you grow up?" And we answer with words such as, "When I grow up, I want to be a doctor. I want to be a teacher. I want to be a farmer."

I've never heard a child say, "When I grow up, I want to be God's son. When I grow up, I want to be God's daughter."

From the earliest of years, what we do gets confused with who we are. So we need to be born *again*. What does it mean to be born *again*? It means we don't have to be like everyone else. It means we get to be like Jesus.

When I grow up, I want to be like Jesus. Jesus was God's Son.

God said, "This is my Son, chosen and marked by my love, delight of my life" (Matt. 3:17 MSG).

You are God's son. You are God's daughter. God is pleased with you.

————

I have a friend who was a little clumsy growing up. When we were in middle school, he showed up for church one Sunday with a cast that began at his hip and ended at the tip of his toes. He was that clumsy. When our Sunday school class let out, we made our way into the auditorium for worship. We were seated in the back row. I was seated at the end of the pew, and he was seated in the middle. When the preacher stood up to preach, my buddy leaned over to the girl sitting next to him and said, "Hey, I need to go to the bathroom."

As everyone started to shift and shuffle their feet for him to make his way out, his cast started banging against the wooden pew in front of us. It sounded as if we were building a house in the back of the sanctuary. By the time he got to me, he was no longer paying attention to walking; rather he was doing damage control with the crowd—nodding, pointing, winking—"Folks, there's nothing to worry about. We've got it under control back here." But then somehow his broken leg got tangled up in my feet.

It wasn't pretty.

He went down like a redwood! Arms flailing. All the women in the church gasped. He hit the ground with the loudest thud you've ever heard.

I did what any good junior high friend would do: I pulled my feet back and acted like nothing had happened, like I was paying attention to the preacher. "Amen, brother! Right on! Preach it!"

The preacher stopped preaching, looked at me, and shrugged his shoulders as if to say, *Are you going to do something for your friend?*

"Get up, dude!" I mumbled under my breath. Compassion was high on my list of spiritual gifts as a thirteen-year-old.

He mumbled something back to me, but I couldn't understand him.

"No, seriously, dude, everyone is looking at us. Get up!" I said out of the side of my mouth.

Still facedown on the ground, he cocked his head to the side and said, "Jon, I can't get up. My braces are caught in the carpet!"

*Oh my.*

I got down to get a better view of the situation. "With one good tug of your head, you should be home free," I said. If you've ever seen the movie *Dumb and Dumber*, it is based on a true story. He was Dumb. I was Dumber.

He took my advice. And with one good yank of his noggin, he pulled free from the fibrous flooring and jumped to his feet. When he waved to the crowd, he also smiled, revealing a huge chunk of red carpet stuck in his teeth.

I tell you that to tell you this: I am spiritually clumsy.

There are days when I trip over my own feet, stumbling and falling and feeling like the whole world is watching me. Sometimes I even feel stuck. Have you ever felt stuck? Maybe you feel stuck in a relationship. Maybe you feel stuck in an occupation. Maybe you feel stuck in a bad habit.

The reason God wants you to be His son or daughter is that He wants you to be free. Free from pressure. Free from worry. Free from comparison. Free from sin.

Free to be . . . you.

Who you are is not determined by what you do. Who you

are is determined by whose you are. You were adopted by God. You are His chosen child. You were handcrafted and handpicked.

Jesus told Nicodemus, "For God so loved the world that He gave His only begotten Son" (John 3:16 NKJV).

God gave His Son so Nicodemus could become a son— born again.

Nicodemus helped Joseph of Arimathea remove Jesus' body from the cross. He went to Jesus at night, only to be associated with Him by day. He went to Jesus as a skeptic, only to become a follower. He went to Jesus as a sinner, only to become a son.

Born again.

————————

I was twelve when I went to Jesus. It doesn't matter when you go to Jesus as long as you go to Jesus.

I stood in the cold waters of Grindstone Creek, and I said, "I believe, with all my heart, that Jesus is the Christ, the Son of the Living God." And with that confession, my dad buried me in the water and raised me out of the water. Dead to sin. Alive in Christ.

Born October 21, 1973. Born again March 30, 1986.

Free to be . . . me. The me God created me to be.

Who will you be?

Better question . . .

Whose will you be?

# THREE

## see (v.)

My dad died of cancer.

I hate cancer. I love my dad.

Although the cancer ravaged his mouth and throat, it did not lay hold of his mind and his heart, nor did it blur his vision.

One afternoon I was sitting beside him and feeding him ice chips when I noticed his eyes were moving around a lot. He smiled several times, so finally I looked around the family room and asked, "Dad, what do you see?" He could only whisper, so I leaned in.

He said, "You don't see them?"

I looked around the room again. From my perspective the room was empty. I said, "No, Dad, I don't see them. What do you see?"

He pulled me close and said, "Jon, there are children everywhere."

We both started to cry.

"Tell me, Dad, what do they look like?" I asked.

In spite of the pain, he smiled from ear to ear and said, "Son, they're so beautiful and so full of life."

A few hours later and just a few hours away from his death, he looked past all of us seated at the table and fixed his eyes on my mom, who was washing dishes at the kitchen sink. He said to her, "Carol, do you feel that?"

She turned off the water and dried her hands with a dish towel. "Feel what?" she asked.

"The two hands in the middle of your back," he said.

My siblings and I stopped what we were doing as he smiled at my mom and said, "He's holding you. He knows you're weak, He knows you're tired, and He just wants you to know that He's strong enough for both of you."

Jesus said, "Blessed are the pure in heart, for they will see God" (Matt. 5:8). It takes a holy heart to see a holy God. I want both. I want a holy heart, and I want to see God.

I heard an ophthalmologist say that there are more nearsighted people in New York City than any other city in our country. Because of all the tall buildings, residents are hemmed in and their fields of vision are limited to short distances. They rarely have to use their sight for long distances, so their eyes adjust and grow accustomed to looking at what is right in front of them.

Too often spiritual nearsightedness limits what I see and how far I see.

And more importantly, *who* I see.

———————

One morning when I was teaching in Haiti, I asked my students to close their eyes and put their heads down on their desks. With the finite means of language, I attempted to paint a picture of the infinite beauty of heaven. Afterward I had my students raise their heads from their desks, and one little girl who shared a bed with five siblings each night asked, "Mr. Jon, will I have my own bed in heaven?"

My response? "Absolutely!"

Another little girl who came to school undernourished asked, "Will we get to eat whatever we want in heaven?"

My response? "Absolutely!"

And one little boy in the back whose dad had drowned and whose mom had died in a fire said, "I want to see Him! I want to see Jesus!"

"Me too."

I want to see Jesus.

Paul said, "Live by faith, not by sight" (2 Cor. 5:7).

Few verses in the Bible are more challenging for me than that one. And even fewer things will limit our fields of vision and create spiritual nearsightedness more than sin. Typically what blocks my view of God is my sin. I squint, I close my eyes, and instead of seeing God, I see what I've done to disobey Him. What I see in front of me is my sin staring back at me.

I have days when I think my sin disqualifies me from seeing God.

There is a thin membrane that separates heaven from earth. We are called to keep our eyes fixed on Jesus in heaven with our feet planted in the soil of earth.

When I turn on the television and all I see are school shootings and terrorist attacks and Amber alerts—when I am surrounded by sin (mine and others'), I sometimes have to stand on my tiptoes to see heaven. It's hard to see above it all.

Whales spend the majority of their time under the surface of the water, but they rely on the air above the surface of the water to survive. We are similar creatures in that we live in one reality but need another reality to sustain us. When the Bible says "walk by faith, not by sight," something in me wants to know where I'm going to land before I jump. I am not alone in that, and neither are you.

Jesus invited a fisherman named Peter to follow Him, and Peter said, "Go away from me, Lord. I'm a sinful man" (Luke 5:8). What Jesus wanted Peter to see is the same thing Jesus sees in you: potential. What Jesus sees in you is not what you see in you.

Peter eventually set down his net to follow Jesus, but that was the easiest thing Peter had to set down. Late one night Jesus invited Peter to let go of fear. Fear will keep us from living by faith because fear is the opposite of faith.

Jesus was walking on water when He invited Peter to join Him. "Come," He said. And Peter went.

I can hear the other disciples pleading with him to stay in the boat, but Peter was beginning to see what Jesus sees: that a life of faith is the best life. So Peter got out of the boat.

There are many boats that we can stay in. There are many boats we can hide in. There are many boats people want to keep us in. But there is only one opportunity to walk on water. I want to see you walk on water. And so does Jesus.

————

Last summer I helped coach my son's baseball team, and we traveled to play in several tournaments. One weekend we stayed in a rough hotel. The TV was chained to the wall, and the smell of cigarette smoke wafted from the vents. You won't find this hotel on Travelocity. My wife told our kids, "Keep your clothes and shoes on, and sleep on top of the blankets."

Our team was swimming in the pool, so I went out to join them and ended up sitting between two highly intoxicated men who weren't with our team. Had I asked them to touch their noses with their fingers, they would have hit their Adam's apples. About an hour into the conversation with them, I learned they were on the run from the police; and the more inebriated they became, the more they opened up to me about their drug-dealing business. At one point one of the men raised his arm up in the air revealing a big, gaping hole where an armpit should have been.

"Yep, my old lady stabbed me," he said.

Not to be outdone, the other man pulled up his shirt to reveal that he had been shot with a shotgun. He didn't have a belly button.

I rolled up my pant leg and said, "I wrecked my bike in the fifth grade."

They laughed and offered to give me something to make the pain go away.

"Thanks, but no thanks!" I said. If I take an Advil, I need a designated driver. What LSD was to Timothy Leary, Benadryl is to me.

Toward the end of the conversation, the talkative one looked at me with a very sincere expression and said, "What do you think we should do?"

My first thought was, *Please don't kill me! I like my armpit and belly button!*

I didn't say what I was thinking.

I know you can't hide and heal at the same time so I said, "Hiding is not living. You need to turn yourselves in."

There was so much pain and regret lingering over our conversation. I wished I could dial back the clock to see what their childhoods had been like or when and where in life they had gotten offtrack. I gave them my phone number and told them, "Who you are today is not who you have to be tomorrow."

And that's when he said it. His eyes were bloodshot and glazed over, but his words were somber. "I can't see that far," he said. "I wish I could, but I can't."

What we see is your past. What Jesus sees is your future.

Jesus is motioning you to follow Him. Jesus is motioning you to trust Him. Jesus is motioning you to run from your past and toward your future.

Jesus did the same to Peter. He invited Peter into a future that Peter couldn't see. Imagine Jesus inviting you to walk on water. Can you blame Peter for looking down? When Peter took his eyes off Jesus, he sank. With his own eyes, Peter saw Jesus raise Lazarus from the dead. With his own eyes, Peter saw Jesus take the sack lunch of a little boy and feed thousands of hungry people. With his own eyes, Peter saw Jesus use mud to heal the eyes of a blind man.

But Peter took his eyes off Jesus.

When we take our eyes off Jesus, we lose our vision.

Have you ever lost sight of what matters?

I have. For me, it's more than just taking my eyes off Jesus. For me, it's when my eyes are on me and only me that I lose sight of what matters and who matters. In fact, when my eyes are on me, I lose sight of Jesus and everyone else.

There's a reason why God designed our eyes the way He did. Our eyes look up and down. Our eyes look side to side and straight ahead. But our eyes don't look inward. And our eyes don't look backward.

That's a good thing.

God wants us to see people the way He sees people. God's eyes are always on people. God doesn't spend hours a day in front of a mirror. God holds a mirror and helps people see what He sees, which is potential. God helps them see what is in front of them, not what is behind them.

God looks through the windshield while we look in the rearview mirror.

———

I was driving through St. Louis when I got stuck in rush-hour traffic. I was in the middle of a six-lane highway. Everywhere I looked there were cars. Big cars. Little cars. No car was moving. Every car stood still. Two hours earlier I had stopped at a gas station in Illinois to buy a Mountain Dew. I bought an industrial-size barrel of the beverage to keep me awake—sixty-four ounces, to be exact. The only problem was God gave me a sixteen-ounce bladder. You do the math.

Contrary to the commercial jingle, I wasn't "Doing the Dew." The Dew was having its way with me. Four hours—that's how long I held it. Four long hours! I'm pretty sure I'll be a candidate for adult diapers in my midforties. I pulled off the highway, ran into a bathroom at a busy outlet mall, and took care of business; and it wasn't until I was at the sink washing my hands that I realized the bathroom didn't have any urinals. Wall-to-wall stalls with doors. *I've never been in a men's bathroom like this before*, I thought to myself.

Then I noticed the floral wallpaper. It still wasn't registering. Then I looked in the mirror. When I looked in the mirror I saw a group of older Asian women staring at me with mortified looks on their faces. As I was drying my hands at the hand dryer—yes, I actually took the time to dry my hands—I said, "Welcome to the United States."

If only Lee Greenwood had been there to sing "God Bless the USA!"

He wasn't.

I didn't think I should stick around long enough to tell them to shop at the Gap, so I left.

Ever been in the wrong place at the wrong time?

Peter was. He never dreamed he would see what he was seeing. Jesus was being beaten by an angry mob when someone pointed to Peter and said, "He's with Jesus!"

Peter shook his head and said, "I don't know the man" (Matt. 26:72). Not once, not twice, but three times. When Jesus needed him the most, Peter denied ever knowing Him. Peter didn't just take his eyes off Jesus; Peter closed his eyes. But Peter didn't need his eyes to hear the rooster crow three times.

I bet Peter wanted to kill that rooster.

The Bible says Jesus "looked straight at Peter" (Luke 22:61). I doubt Peter looked straight at Jesus. Even then, Jesus didn't see failure when He looked at Peter. Jesus saw potential. Even then, Jesus didn't see Peter's past. Jesus saw Peter's future. Jesus saw all the people Peter could help.

That's what Jesus sees when He looks at you. When Jesus sees you, He sees all the people you could help if you could just get your eyes off of you. Instead of looking in a mirror, hold a mirror for others. Help people see beyond their pasts and toward their futures.

———————

In 1982 I was seated in the basement of my parents' house with my two older brothers, watching an epic college basketball game between Georgetown and North Carolina. The game was down to the wire: North Carolina was ahead by a basket with just a few seconds left on the clock. Georgetown called a time-out to draw up one last play.

The ball was given to Georgetown's point guard Freddy Brown. Brown dribbled the length of the court, faked a pass to a teammate, and then did something few will ever forget. He passed the ball to an open player—but the player was on the opposing team. James Worthy of North Carolina intercepted the pass and dribbled the opposite direction until time ran out.

Game over.

North Carolina won. Georgetown lost.

The cameras focused on Freddy Brown, who collapsed on the bench, covered his head with a towel, and began to cry. He thought he had let his team down. He thought he had let his coach down. He thought he had let the fans down.

Failure.

His coach, the legendary John Thompson, came up, put his arm around him, and whispered something comforting in his ear. It was going to be okay.

After His resurrection, Jesus found Peter where He'd found him three years earlier—fishing. This time, Peter didn't say,

"Go away from me, Lord. I'm a sinful man." This time, Peter jumped out of his boat and swam to shore. Out of breath, heart pounding, dripping with water, you know he wanted to say, "Jesus, I'm sorry! Jesus, if I could do it all over again, I wouldn't have denied You!"

Jesus didn't even let him get the words out. Instead Jesus asked, "Peter, do you love Me?"

"Yes, Jesus, You know that I love You!" Peter blurted out.

Not once, not twice, but three times Jesus asked and Peter answered.

It was Jesus' way of saying, "Peter, if that's the worst thing you do in this life, you've got a great life ahead of you."

I have a friend who struggled with same-sex attraction for years. He told me recently, "I misplaced myself for a decade." But then he met Jesus.

I have a friend who aborted three babies in college. She told me recently, "I did things I never dreamed I would do. I became someone I never dreamed I would become." But then she met Jesus.

It's the old line from the old hymn: "I was blind but now I see." Both my friends are now helping their friends see Jesus.

Your past does not define your future.

When God sees you, He doesn't see your sin.

When God sees you, He sees His Son.

And God wants to use you in the same effective way that He used Jesus and Peter.

Once Peter dried off, he stood up in front of thousands of people and helped them see Jesus. Three thousand people saw Jesus clearly that day. Three thousand people were saved that day. Three thousand real people with real problems got real help.

Do you know anyone who has a real problem, who needs real help? God wants you to see all the people you could help. God wants you to see the one person you could help today. Who do you know that is sinking? Who do you know that is on the brink of going under and could use a hand? Who do you know that is walking by sight and not by faith?

Set this book down and call that person.

Set this book down and go see that person.

In the hospital, in the prison, in the nursing home, in your office, down the hallway in your dorm, across the street from your house, or halfway around the world—wherever that person is, is where you need to be.

Go see that person face-to-face so he or she can see Jesus in you.

If you want to see Jesus, you'll find Him where we always find Him: wherever people are hurting, that's where Jesus is.

You need hurting people, and hurting people need you.

They'll see Jesus in you. You'll see Jesus in them.

Set this book down . . .

# FOUR

## die (v.)

Allison and I were in a restaurant eating lunch when an older couple came into the section where we were seated. They were probably in their late seventies, and he was pushing his wife in a wheelchair. It looked as though she had suffered a stroke.

After the waiter set the menus down on our table, we both watched as the husband knelt down in front of his wife, gently holding her hands, and spoke to her with a smile on his face. It was as though they were the only two people in the restaurant. He didn't seem concerned with anyone other than his wife.

He put the brake on the wheelchair, then he scooped her motionless body out of the chair and set her down in the booth. He situated her napkin, plate, and silverware where she could reach them. When her food came, he cut it up and fed it to her; and from time to time, he got up from the table to wipe her mouth. At one point during the meal, I watched him lean across the table, take hold of his wife's hand, and smile at her as he spoke to her.

Tears rolled down her cheeks.

"What do you think he's saying to her?" Allison asked.

"For richer, for poorer . . . in sickness and in health . . . till death do we part," I said.

Tears filled our eyes as we imagined how long they had been married and all they had been through together. And yet it seemed as though they were on their first date.

When we die to self, we give life to others.

Relationships rise and fall based on each person's willingness or unwillingness to die to self. Relationships rise when a person is selfless. Relationships fall when a person is selfish. No one modeled this better than Jesus. Jesus is the standard by which all selfless behavior is measured—He died so we could live.

One day Jesus walked twenty miles out of His way to give life to someone. While the disciples went into town to buy lunch, Jesus sat down at the base of Jacob's Well—the ancient world's version of 7-Eleven. As He pulled out His handkerchief and wiped His brow, a young woman approached with a jar on her head to draw water from the well. Jesus looked overhead and realized it was noon.

Most women drew water from the well during the early morning hours, when the temperature was cool. It was a social event for the women at the start of a day. You didn't draw water alone, during the hottest part of the day, unless no one wanted to be seen with you or you didn't want to be seen with anyone.

"Will you give me a drink?" Jesus asked her.

Her jar nearly fell off her head. Jesus was a Jewish man, and she was a Samaritan woman. Jews and Samaritans didn't speak to one another. Men and women didn't speak to one another. And they definitely didn't drink out of the same glass. As the conversation continued, Jesus moved from casual subjects to intimate subjects, knowing this woman had been wounded by men.

"Go, call your husband and come back," Jesus told her.

"I have no husband," she replied.

Jesus had opened a kitchen cabinet that she'd wanted to keep closed.

"You are right when you say you have no husband. The fact is, you have had five husbands, and the man you now have is not your husband," He said.

When the conversation ended, she kicked off her shoes, ran into town, and said to everyone, "Come meet the man who told me everything I've ever done."

That one line has always struck me as strange. Would you be excited to tell your friends about a man who could tell your friends everything you've ever done? I wouldn't want my friends knowing everything I've ever done.

Jesus obviously didn't look at her the way other men had looked at her. Jesus obviously didn't treat her the way other men had treated her. Jesus died to self so dying people could find life. And when dying people find life, they get excited about it. It's a pattern for relationships that our self-centered world desperately needs.

———————

Years ago, I performed a wedding ceremony for one of my cousins on the first hole of a luxury golf resort in Phoenix, Arizona. After the reception I returned to my bungalow and discovered it had an outdoor bathtub surrounded by a seven-foot-high privacy fence. It had been a long day and I was tired, so I turned it on and crawled in.

As I soaked in the bathtub, I looked up and realized I was surrounded by warm desert air, mountains, a giant cactus, and a sky full of stars. I thought, *This is how Adam felt in the garden of Eden.* God and a naked man communing in the splendor of creation together!

As I got out of the bathtub, I realized I had forgotten a towel. All I had brought outside with me was a washcloth. So I went to open the sliding glass door that led into the room, but it would not open. Some fool had locked it. That fool would be me! I laughed (nervously) and started to feel what Adam felt in the garden when he realized he was naked—*shame.*

Adam had a fig leaf. I had a washcloth.

I climbed over the seven feet of privacy fence (that's a chapter in and of itself) and ran across a fairway to the main lodge. Trying to avoid headlights and a small group of people standing outside drinking cocktails, I hid in a row of bushes for a solid hour. When an employee of the resort walked by, I popped up and motioned to him to help me. But he just laughed and kept walking! He knew I couldn't tip him.

I swallowed my pride and walked into the main lobby with nothing but my birthday suit and washcloth. In high school I had run down a sidewalk in Manhattan, Kansas, wearing nothing but boxers and a ski mask. But this was new territory for this tall and skinny white guy.

I asked the man behind the desk for a key—and whatever training video management had used to prepare him for his job was effective, because he made eye contact the whole time and never flinched as he handed me a new one. As I was walking out of the lobby, there was an older couple walking in. My mom always taught me to hold the door for people so I actually held the door for them. The man laughed, but the woman shot me a look that said, *Pervert!*

"Don't mind me," I said. "I'm just a preacher from Kentucky!"

If we let it, humiliation can lead to humility. Humility is required for submission. *Submission* is the word the Bible uses to describe death to self in a relationship. Paul put it this way: "Do nothing out of selfish ambition or vain conceit, but in humility consider others better than yourselves" (Phil. 2:3).

Jesus treated people better than people treated Jesus. That's why people love Jesus. That's why people die for Jesus. It's easy to die for someone who died for you.

Think about what could happen in your relationships with your spouse, your children, your friends, your coworkers, if you treated them better than they treat you. Think about the life that would be infused into your relationships if you died to self the way Jesus died to self.

Jesus went out of His way to infuse life into the life of the wounded woman at the well. She saw Jesus as an enemy, but Jesus didn't have any enemies. And Jesus commands us not to have any enemies.

The way we make an enemy a friend is by treating them better than they treat us.

There was a violent young boy named Marc in the school where I taught in Haiti. I saw him hit a female teacher one morning, so I intervened on her behalf; and as I pulled him away, he bit through my hand. Responding instead of reacting is never easy in moments like that. I wrapped him up and picked him up, demobilizing his arms. As I carried him out of the school, he kicked me repeatedly and attempted to head butt me.

Carmen, a friend of mine, is the director of the school, so I took Marc to her office. When I set him down, he calmed down. As a teacher, I had a front-row seat that day to a lesson I will never forget. God used Carmen to teach me about death to self.

Carmen didn't say anything to Marc. Instead she went outside, bought some fruit, and brought it back into her office. I watched as she cut it up, placed it in a bowl, and handed it to him. Tears streamed down his cheeks and mine as he devoured it. Marc wasn't an enemy. Marc was a hungry kid. And Carmen treated him better than he was treating us.

Jesus knew the relational storms the woman at the well had weathered in her life, but we don't always know if the people we meet have been dented and dinged by an emotional hailstorm or if they're drowning in a tidal wave of physical abuse. We do know the majority of the people we rub shoulders with each day have boarded up their hearts for one painful reason or another.

---

When I was a kid, I really wanted a Dallas Cowboys winter coat from the J. C. Penney catalog. My parents surprised me one Christmas by giving me one. I put it on with great pride and went outside to test it on a cold Midwestern morning. My brother Jud followed me into the backyard with his Christmas gift—a BB gun.

I stood in the middle of the backyard, and Jud stood twenty feet away. He told me to close my eyes and stick out my arms. Being the younger brother, I did what I was told.

He shot at me.

"Did you feel that?" he asked.

I didn't feel anything, so I shook my head. He shot me again. And again, I didn't feel anything.

"Run from one end of the yard to another. I want to shoot at a moving target," he said.

In ankle-deep snow, I ran from one maple tree to the next while my brother took target practice. A few hours later, when we went in the garage to remove all our wet clothes, Jud turned on the lights. That's when we saw it—dozens of little, round holes all over my new coat. Roger Staubach would not have been happy.

Jud immediately went into damage-control mode. "Take it off, hide it in your backpack, and don't let Mom see it."

There is a basic rule that governs most American households: you can't fool Mom. My mom eventually found my coat. Then she found me. Then she found my brother's backside. My mom couldn't have picked Roger Staubach out of a lineup of older women, but she was madder than Roger Staubach ever would have been.

Some people try to hide the holes in their hearts the way I tried to hide my jacket. But the light of God's grace and truth exposes what we try to hide. Many of the holes we have in our hearts are from words people shot at us.

"You're fat."

"You're ugly."

"You're stupid."

I know my words have wounded people. Someone wise once told me, "Jon, it only takes a year to learn how to talk. But it takes a lifetime to learn what to say."

Jesus' words never wounded people; Jesus' words helped people. Just ask the woman at the well.

————————

I preached on forgiveness recently, and in the process of preparing the sermon I sensed the Holy Spirit prodding me to seek forgiveness from people I had wounded with my words. Most of the names that flooded my memory were from my years in middle school and high school. So I made a list and started collecting addresses and phone numbers.

One by one, I called them and wrote to them. In each exchange I reintroduced myself because I am not the person I once was. I explained that Jesus has forgiven me and asked each person to forgive me. Some did. Some didn't. It was a humiliating experience.

I do not want to wound more people. I want to help more people. I'm learning that a lot of the words that form in my head need to die before they make it to my mouth. My mom, the football expert, is an expert on being selfless.

She used to say, "Jon, if you don't have anything nice to say, don't say anything at all."

What once made me roll my eyes has opened my eyes.

The alarm on my phone rings at 3:16 every day in honor of John 3:16. Jesus died so I can live. So at 3:16 every day I send a text or an e-mail to someone I know, letting them know that I love them.

The more I die to self, the more life I give to others.

Go out of your way to say something nice to someone today.

FIVE

# talk (v.)

A few summers ago I headed to a camp in Colorado to speak to a few thousand teenagers. I didn't have time during the week to prepare my sermon, so I was counting on the flight from Lexington to Denver to put it together.

I sat down between a young couple. The mom was holding a two-year-old boy who looked like the Gerber baby, but as the plane took off the little boy screamed at the top of his lungs—ear piercing, in stereo! Everyone on the flight was getting irritated, and they looked at me thinking he was *my* son because I was seated next to his mom.

About ten minutes into the flight, I leaned over with a smile on my face and said to the mom, "My son does the same thing when we fly. When we give him a sucker, it helps. Do you have a sucker?"

The mom rolled her eyes and said, "We don't feed Sebastian anything unless it's organic."

If your name is Sebastian, we love you but we feel sorry for you.

Trying to lighten the mood, I said, "Do they make broccoli or potato flavored suckers?"

Wow! If looks could kill!

"Do you want to hold him?" she asked.

That was not the response I was expecting. I looked at the dad, but he just shrugged his shoulders and in a real surfer tone said, "Go for it, dude!"

I reluctantly picked up screaming Sebastian, who must have weighed about sixty pounds—that organic diet was treating him right—and he immediately stopped crying. He was on my lap facing me, and when he looked at me and smiled I thought, *What a cute kid with incompetent parents!*

Then, in the blink of an eye, Sumo Sebastian took hold of my hair and pulled like he was weeding a garden. As I pried his man-hands off my head, his dad leaned over and said, "He's a real piston, isn't he?"

"Yeah, he's a real . . . something, all right!" I said.

I don't know if *piston* was the word I would have chosen. His mom started feeding him tiny organic crackers that smelled like a mixture of cat food and multivitamins condensed into wafers. And before I could stop him, he took a handful of it and smeared it all over my laptop, face, and shirt. Sebastian almost met Jesus that day.

We arrived in Denver an hour late. I jumped in the rental car smelling like catfish bait, drove like a NASCAR driver to the camp, pulled into the parking lot, and couldn't find a parking space. In frustration I parked the car on a sidewalk next to a red fire hydrant. There was a sign next to the fire hydrant that said All Cars Will Be Towed At Owner's Expense.

The Holy Spirit told me, "Jon, you don't own this car—Hertz does!" So I left it there.

I walked onstage as the worship leader played the last chorus of the last song. Not only was I out of breath from running, but I didn't have a sermon to preach. There I stood—two thousand students, butterflies in my stomach, tall pine trees reaching toward a star-filled sky, snow-capped mountains in the distance—and I prayed, "Father, tell me what to say and I'll say it."

I told them about Jesus.

An hour later I found myself standing in a cold creek baptizing hundreds of students. When it was all over, I was speechless. I caught a red-eye flight back to Kentucky. I pulled in the church parking lot, exhausted. As I walked into the office area, a woman named Mary Helen stopped me.

"Jon, something weird happened to me last night," she said with a curious smile on her face.

"Really? Tell me about it," I replied.

"Well, God woke me up last night to pray for you." Then she hesitated.

"And . . ." I said in a prodding way.

"I got down on my knees and asked God to speak to me, and He didn't say anything. But He did put a picture in my mind," she said.

"What was the picture of?" I asked.

"It was so weird! You're going to think I'm crazy, but all I could see in the picture was a fire hydrant," she said as she shrugged her shoulders.

I smiled.

Mary Helen smiled back and said, "So I spent the next hour asking God to cover whatever you were doing with the cleansing and purifying water of His Spirit."

I didn't have the heart to tell her that I had parked illegally by a fire hydrant. But I did tell her that her prayers were answered. Before we talk to people about God, we need to talk to God about people.

Prayer is talking to God, and prayer is God talking to us.

There is one topic that should dominate our conversation with God: people we know who don't know God. God wants to talk to us about those people. And God wants us to talk to those people about Him.

———————

The Bible says Zacchaeus was short. Some prefer the term *vertically challenged*. I am *conversationally challenged*. I am an introvert by nature. As a kid I battled shyness. The idea of getting up in front of a crowd was paralyzing for me, so I was content letting others talk for me. Not much has changed. Most people who meet me say, "Jon is reserved." I like that word—*reserved*. I reserve the right not to talk. Most of my friends are not reserved. Most of my friends love to talk. And I love listening to them.

In college I had a friend named Scott who talked to everyone. Every restaurant and every theater we went in, Scott would stand on a chair and say, "Can I get everyone's attention?" He loved being the center of attention. He would then say, "We have a birthday boy in the room today!" And he would have everyone sing "Happy Birthday" to me.

I've had more birthday parties than Methuselah. (If you don't know who that is, look him up.) I was standing behind an eighty-year-old woman in a McDonald's one time when Scott reached around me and goosed her. When she spun around, Scott was long gone, and I was standing there with my mouth wide open. The only words that came out were, "I'm sorry, I don't know what came over me!"

Her eyebrows went up and down, and she smiled as if to say, *Don't let age be a factor!*

I lost my appetite and got out of line.

At a college football game, we were standing in line with hundreds of other men in a crowded bathroom when Scott suddenly turned around, kissed me, shoved me into the men behind me, said, "Jon, I'm not that kind of guy!" and stormed out. Once again, I was left standing there not knowing what to say with several frowning men staring at me.

Jeremiah told God, "I do not know how to speak. I am only a child" (Jer. 1:6).

God answered, "I have put my words in your mouth" (v. 9).

I can relate to Jeremiah. It's not that I don't want to talk—I just don't want to say the wrong things. So I pray, "God, touch my mouth and put Your words in my mouth."

And He does. And what God does for me He can do for you. God can help you talk. Moses stuttered when he talked, but God spoke through Moses. Esther was scared when she talked, but God spoke through Esther. God spoke through fishermen, prisoners, widows, soldiers, shepherds, and teenagers.

God says extraordinary things through ordinary people.

My dad was one of those ordinary people.

Every day my dad prayed that God would put three people in his path that he could talk with about God. God never failed in answering that prayer. One day my dad was driving home from work when he saw a farmer in a field motioning to my dad to turn down the country lane. So my dad did. He got out of his car, walked onto the front porch of the small farmhouse, and before he could knock on the door, a large man in overalls came to the door.

"Did God send you to talk to me?" the man asked.

"Yes, He did," my dad said.

The man invited my dad into the house. As my dad sat down on the couch, he noticed a shotgun on the coffee table.

"I was sitting here with my shotgun trying to think of one reason why I should live another day," the man said in a defeated tone.

"I can give you a good reason. God loves you, and I do too," my dad said back.

The man broke down. His life had been hard. He had more problems than friends. By the end of the afternoon, my dad was his friend. By the end of the evening, Jesus was his friend.

My dad had thousands of conversations like that one. My dad had thousands of friends who became friends with Jesus. Like Jesus, my dad loved to talk with people— people like Zacchaeus.

In one way, Zacchaeus was the Bernie Madoff of his day because he milked people of all their money. In another way, Zacchaeus was the Danny DeVito of his day because he was too short to see above a crowd of people. Imagine the wealthiest man in Jericho running ahead of the crowds to climb a tree in a designer suit.

Two cultural notes about wealthy first-century Jewish men: they didn't run anywhere, and they didn't climb anything. Two observations about why Zacchaeus ran and why Zacchaeus climbed: he wanted to see Jesus, and he didn't want Jesus to see him. So you can imagine his shock when Jesus called him by name and said, "I must come to your house today" (Luke 19:5).

Jesus considered Zacchaeus to be a friend long before Zacchaeus considered Jesus to be a friend.

The Bible says Zacchaeus climbed down quickly. That tells me Zacchaeus didn't have any friends. Zacchaeus ate well. But Zacchaeus ate alone. Jesus didn't see a man who had embezzled millions of dollars. Jesus saw a man in need of love. Jesus saw a lonely man who needed a friend—the kind of friend who would sit down and enjoy a glass of sweet tea with him.

Jesus was at His best when food was put on a table and feet were put under a table.

———

I was standing at our kitchen table making myself a peanut butter and jelly sandwich when I heard what sounded like a professional wrestling match taking place in my daughter's bedroom. On any given day that wouldn't be an unusual occurrence, except on this day I was home alone. With a butter knife in my hand, I stood in the hallway and shouted, "Whoever is in my house needs to leave!"

As soon as the words came out of my mouth, the noise stopped for a moment. That freaked me out even more. That meant whoever was in my house was listening to me! So I ran into my son's bedroom and grabbed his baseball bat. Butter knife in one hand and baseball bat in the other, I yelled again, "Whoever is in my house needs to leave!"

Once again the noise stopped.

As I stood in the hallway holding a Louisville Slugger, I thought, *As a pastor, am I really going to beat someone up with a baseball bat? In the name of the Father, the Son, and the Holy Spirit, I now send you to the ICU!*

As I was having this conversation with my conscience, the commotion started back up and I could hear the shelves and books in Ava's room hitting the floor. It sounded as though someone were pulling her closet door off its hinges and ripping her window blinds off the wall. I was wigged out! I decided to just run into Ava's bedroom swinging my bat. The closer I got, the noise got louder and louder and my heart beat faster and faster.

As I ran into the room, I didn't see two hardened criminals ransacking my daughter's room. What I did see were three of the largest crows you could ever imagine trying to find a way out of my house. I felt like a character in a short story by Edgar Allan Poe. I still don't know how the birds got there or who put them there.

As I tried to open some windows to let them out, they dive-bombed me—hitting me in the back of the head and clawing at my shirt. I thought, *I'm going to be abducted by one of these pterodactyls!* Then one of them landed on Ava's bedpost and just stared me down. Like Dirty Harry, it cocked its head to the side as if to say, *Go ahead—make my day!*

Like Babe Ruth, I pointed my bat and said, "Get ready to meet your Maker!"

As I got ready to tee off, it flew into our living room with its other two partners in crime. I opened all the doors in our house and found myself talking to the birds—"The garage door is open! Fly that way! No, that way!"

The birds were like, *Thanks, Dr. Doolittle!*

Twenty minutes later my house was bird-free. As I was lying in bed that night, my sweet and usually supportive wife, Allison, clicked off the light and said, "They were hummingbirds, weren't they?"

I didn't talk to her for a month!

If I'm willing to talk to birds, surely I can talk to God. And if I can talk to God, surely I can talk to people. Evangelism is talking to our friends about our friendship with Jesus.

Jesus told Zacchaeus, "Salvation has come to your house today" (v. 9).

Jesus told everyone else, "I came to seek and to save the lost" (v. 10).

Zacchaeus got taller that day. The family of God got bigger that day.

Who do you know that doesn't know God as a Father and Jesus as a brother? I keep a list of names—people I meet in restaurants, grocery stores, the gym, and doctors' offices. I talk to God about them before I talk to them about God.

People are the focus of my prayers. I pray with regularity and with spontaneity, so I have scheduled and unscheduled times to pray.

The first time I meet a person, I pray for them without them knowing it: "Father, thank You for creating James. Thank You for loving James. Thank You for dying for James. Thank You for allowing me to meet James. Help me to love James the way he needs to be loved today."

I never force the conversation. My friend Gary says, "If it's forced, it's of the flesh. If it flows, it's of the Spirit."

One of the best ways to start a conversation is with a question: Is there anything I can do for you today? When we present ourselves in a loving way to people, people will let us love them. And when people let us love them, usually they'll let us talk about why we love them.

When given permission to talk, keep it simple. Tell your story. "Without Jesus, my life was like this . . . With Jesus, my life is like this . . ."

When given permission to talk, don't be weird. There are enough cheesy Christians in the world today. Be yourself and be normal.

I have a friend named Brian who prayed that God would allow him to fill an entire row of chairs at our church with his friends who didn't know Jesus. Week after week I watched as that row filled up. Year after year I watched as Brian's friends accepted Christ. Nineteen people fell in love with Jesus through riding motorcycles and playing softball with Brian.

Brian would tell you it's not about ability. It's about availability. Brian made himself available to God, and God used Brian to lead his friends to Jesus.

We have a leadership axiom at Southland: We move forward on our knees. We pray about people. As a church family, we want to take as many people to heaven with us as possible. We want heaven to have overcrowding issues because we showed up at the party with more people than expected.

We ran out of room at our church years ago, so we prayed God would give us more space for more people. God gave us a mall. When we first opened, people walked in and said, "I bought a pair of shoes over there." And, "I played in an arcade over there." Now people walk in and say, "My marriage was restored over there." And, "I overcame my addiction to drugs over there."

We had a fistfight in our children's ministry because one boy said something to another boy about his mama. I can't think of a better place for those two boys to be than in a loving environment with loving people.

God gave us a mall because God has a list.

———————

Names matter because people matter. Every name on the planet is on God's list. Including Thomas. I met Thomas on a flight to Las Vegas. I was traveling to speak at a church there, so I had my family with me. Thomas was seated next to me in the aisle seat. I'd never seen someone drink so much alcohol on a flight before. If he said it once, he said it a hundred times: "I work hard so I can play hard."

The more intoxicated he became, the more he commented on how beautiful my wife was. I quickly realized he didn't think I deserved to be married to her. I agree, but I didn't need him to tell me so!

Thomas was wearing a nice suit and had a nice watch, but his language was far from nice. He told me what a young guy like me could do with my free time in Vegas. From gambling to women to drugs, it was apparent that Thomas believed the tourism slogan of "What happens in Vegas stays in Vegas."

I tried to change the subject multiple times. I talked about basketball, fishing, cars, the weather, and I even brought up Wayne Newton! All Thomas wanted to talk about was everything I didn't want to talk about.

I started talking to God about Thomas early in the flight. And with thirty minutes left in the flight, Thomas said, "Do you know what I do for a living?"

"I have no idea," I said.

"I sue preachers for a living." He said it with joy.

It was the first time in my life that I thought about drinking on a flight.

"Really? That sounds interesting," was the only comment I could come up with.

"I love nothing more than taking preachers and their television ministries to the cleaners. I've made millions suing those @#%&*," he said as he raised his glass.

Allison's elbow ran deep into my side. And that's when it happened. I knew it was coming. There was no stopping it.

"And what about you?" Thomas asked. "What do you do for a living?"

My first inclination was to say, "I'm a circus clown. My wife is a trapeze artist. My kids are lion tamers, and we're performing at Caesar's Palace tonight."

Instead, I swallowed hard and said, "I love people for a living."

"You do what?" he said, nearly choking on his bourbon and Coke.

I elaborated. I told him that I get to see children adopted into loving homes, and I get to see hungry people fed, and I get to see the addicted discover sobriety, and I get to see thousands of college students realize there is more to this life than making money. I talked and I talked and I talked, and I talked some more.

I told him about my friend Nathan. Nathan killed a man when he was a teenager, but Nathan knows Jesus now. I told him about my friend Lonnie who was a manager at a strip club, but Lonnie knows Jesus now.

I talked. Thomas listened.

As the plane landed, Thomas said, "I still haven't figured out that making money isn't all there is."

After all I said, that's what he said. I'm expecting a lawsuit soon. I'm okay with it if it would give me another chance to talk to Thomas. As long as Thomas is on God's list, Thomas will stay on my list.

Grace. God has it. People need it.

So start talking and don't ever stop.

## SIX

# rest (v.)

I love spending time in the basement of my house. And even more than that, I love spending time in the basement of my house with my kids. We build forts, we have Nerf gun wars, and we play Ping-Pong. That is how we spend our time in the basement.

My son and I invented a game called Sting Pong. We take off our shirts and as we play a normal game of Ping-Pong, we try to hit each other with the ball in the chest, which results in bonus points. If it leaves a red mark, it's an automatic victory. It's one part barbaric and one part childish, but we love it!

We were in the middle of an epic Sting Pong tournament recently and I said, "Silas, if you lose this next match, you have to run around the house in your underwear."

He laughed and said, "Okay! But, Dad, if you lose, you have to eat one of my toenails!"

"Whoa, whoa, whoa! That's not an even trade," I said.

That's when my elementary-age son came back at me with, "Dad, all's fair in love and war."

I was so impressed he knew that line that I agreed to the terms without giving it much thought. We shook hands and the battle began. And all I want to say is this: I'm just glad my son has small toes. In my defense, when my son plays Sting Pong, he channels his inner Roger Federer. He's unstoppable!

I love spending time in my basement with my kids because life slows down to a manageable pace there. It's as if my basement is a clock-resistant time warp.

Isn't time an interesting reality?

When I'm in the basement with my kids, it's as if time stands still. If I'm anywhere else on the planet, it's as if time flies by. There are some events I go to where I'm surprised by how fast time seems to move, and other events where time isn't moving fast enough.

I don't know if you consistently arrive to scheduled events ten minutes early or if you consistently arrive to scheduled events ten minutes late. American businessman Franklin Jones once said, "The trouble with being punctual is that nobody's there to appreciate it."

When I ask people how they are doing, the two most frequent responses are "I'm busy" and "I'm tired." We live in a society with one-minute rice, one-minute workouts, and one-minute Bible reading plans. We also have instant oatmeal, instant coffee, instant replay in sports, and instant messaging on our computers. We have speed-dialing features on our phones, we can take speed-reading courses in college, and some people even wear Speedos to the beach. (They shouldn't, but they do!)

You would think more conveniences would bring more margin. But none of it has made anyone less busy or less tired. If anything, we are busier and more tired than we've ever been.

Scott Scruggs, teaching pastor of Menlo Park Presbyterian Church, said, "While instant gratification may seem to be going up, lasting contentment is on its way down."

How often do we say to people, "Let's grab lunch or coffee sometime" or "Let's get our families together sometime"? But *sometime* never comes. We don't have time for sometime.

There is a war being waged between two perspectives on time.

The Bible teaches that time is a gift.

Our world teaches that time is money.

For average Americans, God doesn't live in their hearts; He lives on the screens of smartphones. And I feel the tension. I sometimes feel like a hamster in a wheel, as if I'm running more than I'm resting.

I want to believe my life is structured and systematized, ordered and organized. But with all the plates I'm spinning, I am working long hours that turn into long days that turn into long weeks and long months and long years that will eventually cut my life short.

And God is saying, "Jon, *rest*."

I am a noun that needs this verb.

I have been through seasons in life when I haven't slept well. When I don't sleep well, I don't live well. Physical fatigue drains the emotional tank. When your emotional tank is empty, it's hard to be full of anything good. If your marriage has drained you, you're probably full of resentment. If your work has drained you, you're probably full of bitterness. If religion has drained you, you're probably full of confusion.

God doesn't empty anyone. God fills everyone. And God fills everyone with good things like contentment and joy. God uses rest as the pump to fill our tanks.

That's why Jesus said, "Are you tired? Worn out? Burned out on religion? Come to me. Get away with me and you'll recover your life. I'll show you how to take a real rest. Walk with me and work with me—watch how I do it. Learn the unforced rhythms of grace. I won't lay anything heavy or ill-fitting on you. Keep company with me and you'll learn to live freely and lightly" (Matt. 11:28–30 MSG).

*Rest* is a verb that is intentionally void of action. Rest requires inaction. While we rest, God works. That's what makes this verb a challenge to our faith. Do we really believe that God is in control? If we do, we can rest. If we don't believe God is in control, we ask Him to rest while we attempt to do His work.

God made the world in six days and rested on the seventh day. Some people believe God stopped working after that first week, turned the keys to the universe over to us, retired, and is currently collecting a Social Security check each month.

God is still at work.

In my teens, I realized God worked hard to save me. In my twenties, I realized God works hard to keep me saved. In my thirties, I'm realizing I can relax. I can take a deep breath, close my eyes, put my feet up, and live a life of gratitude because God is working harder than ever in my life. And if I were God's only client, He would have to work overtime because of the messes I create. But I know I'm not the only person creating work for God.

I resigned as the manager of the universe several years ago, and I've never slept better. Since turning in my letter of resignation, I've learned to slow down by sitting down.

———

In the heart of downtown Manhattan, right in the middle of the busiest city in the world—amid the maze of skyscrapers and the honking taxis and the people hurrying here and there—are 843 acres we know as Central Park. Forty million people a year spread out picnic blankets, throw Frisbees with their dogs, and enjoy leisurely jogs in the shade of tree-lined trails. But the biggest activity in Central Park each day is nonactivity. Most people come to Central Park to sit down. There are more than nine thousand benches in Central Park.

In the middle of the Bible is God's Central Park, and Psalm 23 is God's park bench.

"The Lord is my shepherd" (Ps. 23:1).

David didn't write, "The Lord is *a* shepherd" or "The Lord is *the* shepherd." David wrote, "The Lord is *my* shepherd."

He lets us have Him. It's not ownership. It's belonging. I am His and He is mine.

Martin Luther said, "The vast majority of the Christian life is about personal pronouns."

And if God is *my* shepherd, that makes me *His* sheep. If you know anything about sheep, that's not a very glamorous distinction, but it is a true one. I have tried to be my own shepherd and that didn't work so well. Like a sheep, my appetite led me into dangerous and even deadly places. I enjoy letting God lead because He leads me away from death and toward life.

"He makes me lie down in green pastures," David wrote (Ps. 23:2).

Psalm 23 doesn't say, "He *asks* me to lie down" or "He *invites* me" or "He *persuades* me." It says, "He *makes* me."

Forced rest.

My friend Dale bought me a hammock and told me he would be very offended if I didn't use it. I tied it between two walnut trees in my backyard, and at least once a week I try to take a nap and not offend Dale. Do you know what a hammock does? A hammock destroys worry. A hammock drives a stake through the heart of anxiety.

You were created to live outside. When was the last time you fell asleep outside? When was the last time you wrapped up in a big blanket and slept with the windows in your bedroom open? Fresh air is good for the soul.

And so is sleep.

If you are busy, behind, buried, or burned-out, one of the most spiritual activities you can engage in is the nonactivity of sleep.

Some friends of mine bought a mattress for a man who couldn't afford a new one after bedbugs destroyed his. He had been sleeping on the same mattress since the early 1970s, which meant he hadn't slept well since the 1990s. He called them the next morning and said, "I haven't slept this well in over twenty years."

Lack of sleep is not an isolated phenomenon. Forced rest is. The US Centers for Disease Control and Prevention estimated that seventy million Americans suffer from some form of insomnia. And what keeps us up at night is stress. More and more people are stressed out.

The word *stressed* spelled backward is *desserts*. Maybe if we ate more desserts we would sleep better! It seems to work for my daughter. She claims she can find all four food groups at Baskin-Robbins. There is something to be said for less stress and more sleep. The more stress I have in my life, the less I sleep.

Chasing a toddler all day is stressful. Being unemployed is stressful. Caring for an aging parent is stressful. Fighting a chronic illness is stressful. Worrying about a prodigal child is stressful. Cancer is stressful. Divorce is stressful. Bankruptcy is stressful. We have a million and one reasons to have more stress and less sleep.

Jesus always seemed to be on the lookout for people who needed less stress and more sleep. One day a man who couldn't walk was lowered through a roof by four of his friends. They wanted their buddy to have an opportunity to be healed by Jesus, but the house where Jesus was teaching was so full of people they couldn't squeeze him in. So they fired up their chain saws and cut a hole in the roof of the house. That tells me the man on the mat had good friends. It also tells me the man on the mat was desperate for help.

We could be the kind of friends who mow a neighbor's yard or babysit for a single mom so she can run errands or anonymously make a mortgage payment for a family that is struggling to make ends meet. We could be the kind of people who alleviate the pressure that creates more stress and prevents our friends from sleeping.

---------

My friend Sam had a friend who was battling depression. His buddy was lonely and sad, so Sam bought a sleeping bag and slept on the floor next to his friend's bed as a sign of support and solidarity. He cooked for his friend, cleaned his apartment, did his laundry, posted Scripture on his bathroom mirror, and prayed out loud for him each morning. It took a month before his friend would leave the apartment, but Sam finally convinced him to eat at a Mexican restaurant with a group of friends.

Everybody benefits from chips and salsa therapy!

Sam didn't cut a hole in the guy's roof, but he did figure out a way to get to his heart. By sleeping next to his bed, Sam helped his friend cut a path to Jesus. And the closer we get to Jesus, the closer we get to rest.

Whenever I have more stress than I have sleep, I ask myself a series of questions:

Is Jesus still on the throne?
Is Jesus' tomb still empty?
Is Jesus coming back to get me?

If the answer to each of those questions is yes, then I can rest.

I heard about a cardiologist who had the chairs in his waiting room reupholstered. When the man finished re-covering each of the chairs with new fabric, he told the doctor, "I only had to replace the material on the seats of the chairs, specifically the edge of the seats."

The doctor looked at the man with a confused look, so the man clarified what he was saying. "It seems that most of your patients sit on the edge of the seat and never lean back, so just the front part of each chair was worn out."

Before the sun goes down today, cut a path to a basement, a bench, a hammock, a Baskin-Robbins, or some chips and salsa.

God is inviting you to lean back and rest.

SEVEN

# turn (v.)

I recently hosted a meeting for church leaders in my office. They were from various churches and nonprofits from around the country, but what they have in common is that I look up to all of them. To be honest, I was nervous about saying or doing something stupid in the meeting to embarrass the church I lead.

We have a fun staff culture at Southland, and we play a lot of practical jokes on one another. In the weeks leading up to the meeting, I may or may not have participated in putting a dead deer on a coworker's desk. Hours before my meeting with this esteemed group of leaders, the coworker who had been blessed with a visit by Bambi's relative had broken into my office, removed a family picture from the wall behind my desk, and replaced it with a portrait of the Jackson 5.

Even though my kids don't have Afros or wear glittery outfits, somehow I never noticed the heist. As I sat with my back to the picture and talked about global leadership development, a handful of sixty-year-old men who lead respected ministries stared at Jermaine, Tito, Marlon, Randy, and Michael.

Back in the day, I loved the Jackson 5, but I'm not so sure they contributed to my credibility as a leader during that meeting. I can think of hundreds of episodes in my life where if I had just turned around I would have saved myself a lot of embarrassment.

The verb *repent* means a change of thinking and implies a turning around of one's life—to walk in a new direction and toward a new destination. "Stop at the crossroads and look around. Ask for the old, godly way, and walk in it. Travel its path, and you will find rest for your souls" (Jer. 6:16 NLT).

The great theologian Dr. Seuss once said, "Wherever you go, there you are." You can't run from yourself. You can't run from God. And where God is, is where you want to be.

There is a lie circulating in our tabloid-ridden culture that says, "All roads lead to God." That's like saying, "All roads lead to Chipotle." I wish all roads led there. That would make my life much easier. But all roads don't lead to Chipotle. As a matter of fact, there are two Chipotle restaurants in the town where I live, and if you want to get to them, you have to take either Nicholasville Road or Richmond Road. So only two roads lead to Chipotle where I live.

The Bible teaches there are two paths in life. There is a path that leads to death. And there is a path that leads to life. Only one of the paths leads to God. I've discovered that picking the right friends helps me pick the right path.

Pick the people who pick the right path, and you will end up in the right place.

––––––––––

I heard someone say one time, "Stupid rubs off."

Some of us have friends who can't finish a sentence without cussing. Can profanity rub off? Absolutely. Some of us work with people who cut corners and put forth the least amount of effort possible. Can laziness rub off? Absolutely. Anger rubs off. Cynicism rubs off. Lots of things you don't want rub off.

"Bad company corrupts good character" (1 Cor. 15:33).

Let's turn the tables. Some of us have friends who start their day by reading their Bible and praying. Can joy rub off? Absolutely. Some of us have friends who are incredibly encouraging with their words. Can kindness rub off? Absolutely. Generosity rubs off. Wisdom rubs off.

Imagine you are standing on top of a tall building when God hands you a rope. Standing on the ground looking up at you is a long line of people, and each person in line is a friend of yours. It would be far easier for them to pull you down to where they are than it would be for you to pull them up to where you are.

During my senior year of high school, my friends convinced me to meet them at the University of Missouri campus for a homecoming parade. I knew better but went anyway. And once I arrived, I regretted it. I saw fraternity and sorority members streaking. I saw several fights. I saw a drunk college student climb an electrical pole and get electrocuted; when the ambulance showed up to help him, the other drunk students flipped it over and broke out its windows.

Leaving my friends there and driving home, I felt sick to my stomach for what I had allowed my heart and mind to be exposed to. I thought I was stronger than I was. I thought I could pull my friends up, but my friends ended up pulling me down.

"Walk with the wise and become wise; associate with fools and get in trouble" (Prov. 13:20 NLT).

––––––––

When I dropped my daughter off for her first day of middle school this year, do you think her greatest concern was getting the best education possible? Do you think she was wondering, *Man, will my teachers have graduate and post-graduate degrees?*

Ava was thinking what every other kid in our country was thinking on the first day of school: *When I sit down in the cafeteria, will anyone be saving a seat for me? Or will I be staring into a sea of strangers?*

Ava has friends she hangs out with and shares secrets with and plays with and talks with. It all comes down to that word *with*. Who will we share our lives with? Companionship matters to kids just as it matters to adults.

One day a group of pious adults pulled a woman out of the bed where she was having an affair with a married man. Jesus was in the temple teaching, and they dragged her in front of Jesus and the crowd to shame her. And there she stood—naked, heart pounding, palms sweating, alone. No one was standing with her. The adults gathered around her, rocks in their hands. By law, she deserved to die, but someone asked Jesus, "What do you say?" (John 8:5).

Good move. When I don't know what to say, I look to see what Jesus had to say. Jesus didn't say anything at first. Instead, He knelt down and with His finger began to write in the dirt. We don't know what He wrote, but my best guess is He wrote the names of the men who were holding rocks and next to their names He named their sins—the sins they deserved to die for.

Why? Because of what He finally said: "If any of you is without sin, let him be the first to throw a stone at her" (John 8:7).

The crowd went silent. And all that could be heard that day was the sound of rocks hitting the ground. One by one, the men left. And Jesus, a loving man, stood face-to-face with a wounded woman and said, "Woman, where are they? Has no one condemned you?"

"No one, sir," she said.

"Then neither do I condemn you," Jesus declared. "Go now and leave your life of sin" (John 8:10–11).

You fall into one of two camps with Jesus: you are either forgivable, or you are forgiven. Anyone who has been shamed by sin is forgivable. If you are a follower of Jesus, you are already forgiven. And to be forgiven means you are set free from the shame of your sin.

Like Jesus, we surround those who have been blistered and burned by their choices. The church was never meant to be a pristine showroom. It was meant to be a messy living room filled with people who have messed up. It isn't a place for finger-pointing and rock throwing.

What flows out of the church is what flows out of Jesus— help, hope, and healing.

Imagine what it was like for that woman hearing the voice of Jesus say, "Neither do I condemn you."

We don't turn our backs on people. We turn toward people, and we help them turn toward God.

In the same way there are two competing paths, there are also two competing voices in this life: "Whether you turn to the right or to the left, your ears will hear a voice behind you, saying, 'This is the way; walk in it'" (Isa. 30:21).

I haven't always listened to the right voice.

———

Every graduating class from the dorm I lived in during college would pass down a photo album. Inside the photo album was a collection of pictures from previous graduating classes posing with the campus security guard. Late at night the security guard would walk through all the buildings on campus with a flashlight, making sure everything was locked up. Then he would drive around campus for an hour and eventually park his car in front of the administration building. Sometime around three o'clock in the morning, he would take a nap. Once he was asleep, we would all gather at his cop car and take what we called a "family portrait" of us all posing with him asleep in his car.

Some would lie on the hood; others would be so bold as to crawl on top of his car. One graduating class tied barnyard animals to his bumper and had a Noah's Ark theme. My class decided that posing on the outside of the car was playing it safe, so we decided to crawl inside the car and snap a family portrait from inside. I drew the short straw, so I had to slide in the front seat first, right next to Barney Fife. Some of my buddies climbed in next to me, while others piled in the backseat.

We all wore wigs and beards and bathrobes—our theme was the Last Supper of Jesus with the twelve apostles. The guys in the back row were all breaking bread, while all of us in the front seat were holding up chalices filled with grape juice.

Jesus, please forgive me!

There we sat—thirteen of us—inside the car with a sleeping security guard who was probably in his midseventies. But when the freshman outside the car snapped the picture, the flash woke up the security guard, and everyone scattered like mad to get out of the car.

But I was stuck! I decided to play it cool. I turned to my left and smiled at him. All I remember saying as I slid out was, "Sir, please don't pepper spray me! Please don't pepper spray me."

Most people go to college to get smart. You would think the smarter we get the less we would sin. People are getting smarter but not wiser. For example, I read in an article from a London newspaper that Dutch psychologists hope to remove the social stigmas from pedophilia and normalize it as a healthy sexual orientation. It was backed up with modern research and lauded as scholarship. But is it wise?

"The wisdom of this world," said Paul, "is foolishness to God" (1 Cor. 3:19 NLT).

Twenty years ago I had to walk away from some friendships to become friends with Jesus. My friends were pulling me down, and I needed a friend who could pull me up. That friend was and still is Jesus. Because of Jesus I can now stand on a roof and pull others up without them pulling me down. Because of Jesus I can now point other people to the path that leads to life—the path that leads to God.

Ben Petrick is a former major league baseball player who had to walk away from a promising career due to Parkinson's disease. After an incredible rookie year with the Colorado Rockies, he noticed stiffness and rigidity in his left hand. Within a few years he lost all mobility and is now completely dependent on his wife to care for him.

"Each day I get a little stronger about being weaker," he told a reporter for ESPN.

Admitting we are weak is the first step in turning our lives around. Admitting that we struggle with lust, gossip, materialism, overeating, lying, pride, selfishness, jealousy, or laziness is the first step in becoming dependent on Jesus.

Dependence on Jesus will make us strong in the face of temptations that make us feel weak.

It's the principle from AA that says, "If you want to go fast, go alone. If you want to go far, go together." We all need friends who will help us turn a weakness into a strength. We all need friends who will walk with us and help us avoid the spiritual potholes that trip us up and keep us down.

Jesus can help us avoid the pit of poor choices. The question is, will we tune and turn our ears toward His voice?

When I was fourteen years old, I heard that voice. I was sitting on the back row in a chapel at a church camp listening to a man preach with passion about making Jesus the Lord of your life. At the end of his message, everyone stood up and we started to sing the old hymn "I Have Decided to Follow Jesus." The preacher offered an invitation to anyone who wanted to let Jesus lead their life. I wanted so badly to respond, but I was deathly shy at the time and was intimidated by the thought of standing up in front of a crowd and making such a bold declaration.

The singing got louder and louder—"No turning back, no turning back." And my heart beat faster and faster. I stood with a death grip on the pew in front of me, feeling as if I had sandbags tied to my feet. I was paralyzed by fear. As the Spirit continued to stir in my heart, the tears started to run down my cheeks, but I couldn't take the step and walk down the aisle.

When the service ended, I walked out of the chapel and made my way to the baseball field on the camp property. As all the campers went to sleep that night, I lay down in the middle of the outfield and looked up at the stars. There are just some nights when the stars seem to be so close you could reach out and touch them. God felt even closer than the stars that night.

I remember turning my palms over and saying, "God, wherever You want me to go and whatever You want me to do, and whoever You want me to love, I'm in . . . I'm all in."

That was a turning point in my life. And in my mind, I return to that night often.

What do you need to turn away from so that you can turn toward Jesus?

With His help and by His grace, may we reach the point of no return.

PART TWO

# *church*—the people (n.) who love (v.) people

## EIGHT

# dance (v.)

My cousin Kathy was born with Down syndrome.

Every year when our family would gather at my grandparents' house in western Kansas, Kathy would set up all the birthday cards she had received the previous year on the kitchen table and explain why each one meant so much to her.

She also loved to show us the engagement ring that her "boyfriend" had given her. The wedding wasn't scheduled for a specific date on the calendar; rather, each year she would tell us, "I'm getting married in fourteen years!" My two older brothers were going to be ushers. I was assigned the distinguished role of ring bearer. But as each year passed, I explained to her that if I had to wait fourteen more years, I might just be the oldest ring bearer in human history! Kathy would laugh and give me one of her signature hugs.

Hugging Kathy made me realize how beautiful life is. Kathy added beauty to this life for forty-eight years. I miss hugging Kathy. It was a privilege. But what I really miss is Kathy hugging me. Someday you'll get to experience a hug from Kathy. I can't imagine heaven would be complete without her welcoming people to the party. And that's ultimately what this idea is about. A party. The party. Where I'm from we call it Jesus Prom.

I wish I could remember my prom night. It was such a blur—a hurried mess of getting dressed, taking pictures, eating out, and hanging out—that I really don't remember much of it. I guess it was too much like every other prom, so I've chosen to forget it. But I haven't forgotten the second prom I went to. I will always remember it. And the reason I will always remember it is because all the people who were never invited to a high school prom were invited to this one.

Beautiful people like my cousin Kathy. Beautiful people like my friend Jenny.

I pay the bills by standing on a stage each weekend and teaching thousands of people to love people. It's a rewarding gig. Jenny sits on the front row each weekend, and after listening to me for ten minutes she usually gets up and goes to the bathroom. It's also a very humbling gig.

During one of my talks Jenny stood up, but instead of walking to the back of the room where the bathrooms are located, she turned to the crowd and motioned for all of them to stand up too. Trust me, I hadn't said anything profound. Jenny just felt led to give me a standing ovation. She started to clap and cheer, and when no one else joined her, she turned around a second time and put both hands on her hips as if to say, *I mean it, people! Get up off your lazy cans and give this man a round of applause!*

Three seconds later I received a standing ovation from three thousand people. I thanked Jenny and she said, "You're welcome, Jon!" Then she stood on her chair, took a bow, and received a round of applause!

Jesus said, "When you put on a luncheon or a banquet, don't invite your friends, brothers, relatives, and rich neighbors. For they will invite you back, and that will be your only reward. Instead, invite the poor, the crippled, the lame, and the blind" (Luke 14:12–13 NLT).

We decided to throw a party for Jenny and her friends. We sent out invitations to physically and mentally challenged people living in our city, and we asked them to come to prom with us. We invited local tuxedo stores and formal dress stores to provide free attire for our guests to wear. And they did! We invited local restaurants to cater the event. And they did! We invited local limousine owners to pick up and deliver our privileged friends. And they did!

We invited tailors and seamstresses to make sure every article of clothing fit as though it had been custom-made for a runway in Paris. Whether they were wheelchair-bound, bent over, or missing a leg—who better to be adorned in the finest of clothing? We rolled out the red carpet and handed hundreds of disposable cameras to middle school students who played the role of the paparazzi. We hung disco balls and strobe lights, then put a live band onstage to cover the best Motown has to offer.

And as thousands of people poured in, something magical happened in the universe. A new normal was defined. A new flavor of love was showcased. A new picture of perfection was captured. If Jesus were anywhere on the planet that night, He would have been in that room on that dance floor cutting a rug with the first-class citizens of Lexington, Kentucky.

Someone more perceptive than I am once observed, "Grace is the face love wears when it meets imperfection." The many people who have put up with me, not given up on me, included me, and helped me, have all looked at me through the lens of grace.

Prom night has changed how I look at people.

Prom night has changed how I look at myself.

Prom night has changed how I look at love.

————

When I was a little boy, my family picked up a man named Charlie and took him to church with us. There were Sundays when I felt like Charlie was taking us to church.

When Charlie's mom had gone to the hospital to deliver him, her doctor was at a Christmas party. He showed up in the delivery room intoxicated and angry because he'd had to leave the party. He pushed on her stomach. It was her first pregnancy, so she didn't know the protocol. She assumed his behavior was standard procedure. But standard medical procedure doesn't take the life of a young mom.

Not only did Charlie never meet the mom who gave him life; Charlie did not receive enough oxygen in the process and was born with cerebral palsy. His mind works, but his body does not. For the first twelve years of Charlie's life, his dad carried him everywhere he needed to go. Charlie's dad is one of the finest men I've ever known.

My family had the privilege of taking Charlie to church every Sunday for more than a decade. We took Charlie until he started telling his friends about his friend Jesus. Our wood-paneled station wagon lacked the seating capacity necessary to get Charlie and his friends from the group home they lived in to church. So we started using the church van—seating capacity, sixteen adults.

By the time I was in high school, the first two rows of my home church were filled by Charlie and his friends. If a man who is considered limited by worldly standards knows enough to talk about Jesus to his friends, then what's my excuse?

Hearing Charlie sing, "Oh, How I Love Jesus," is one of the highlights of my life. I know Jesus loves Charlie. And I know Charlie loves Jesus.

Though I didn't always understand Charlie when he talked, Charlie always understood something I didn't. Everybody's odd but God. That sounds like something you would put on a sign for Cracker Barrel to sell. But it's true. God is the only standard of normal. Everybody except God is challenged.

Jesus met a challenged man. For thirty-eight years the man couldn't walk. His family placed him by a pool in Jerusalem that many believed to have healing powers. When the water was stirred, whoever jumped in first was healed. Obviously, those who couldn't jump, let alone walk or stand up, didn't have a chance.

Jesus asked him, "Do you want to get well?" (John 5:6).

The word for *well* is *whole*. Jesus knew a piece of this man was missing.

A wheelchair is a great invention. But a wheelchair is no replacement for feet. A prosthetic is a great invention. But prosthetics are no replacement for legs. What all the king's men couldn't do for Humpty Dumpty, Jesus wanted to do for this man. And Jesus did. Jesus made him whole again.

What Jesus did for his body that day, Jesus will do for every body someday.

————

I have days when I take my feet and legs for granted.

Each summer I climb a mountain with my brother Jud. He lives in the mountains of Colorado. And I love standing above fourteen thousand feet. The air is thin but the wind is strong. I feel alive on top of a mountain. I also feel small on top of a mountain.

In the Old Testament, God met a lot of people on the tops of mountains. They walked up, and God walked down. In the New Testament, God came all the way down so that someday we could go all the way up. That's what I think about when I'm on top of a mountain.

Last year when we drove into town after our climb, we pulled into a gas station. Parked at the pump next to us was a wheelchair-accessible van. Inside the van was a man who had lost his legs to diabetes. Every movement required extra effort from him. Every action required extra time. With little effort and in little time, I walked in and out of the gas station.

Joni Eareckson Tada lost her mobility as a teenager when she dove into shallow water. For forty-six years she has been confined to a wheelchair. I heard her speak this summer at a conference, and in her message she said, "I'd rather have Jesus and no legs than have legs and not have Jesus."

I could tell she meant what she said. As I walked out of the arena, I wondered if I could say the same thing and mean it.

After Peter and John healed the disabled man by the gate called Beautiful, he went "walking, leaping, and praising God" (Acts 3:8 NLT). In other words, he danced.

There are a lot of things I want to see in heaven. I would like to see Joni Eareckson Tada dance.

Our role is to bring as much of heaven to earth today so that we can take as much of earth to heaven someday. Our role is to get people ready for the dance. Our role is to be someone's dance partner.

————————

Your senior class could make *your* prom *their* prom. The average high school senior spends eleven hundred dollars on prom. What if your class collected and spent its money throwing a party unlike any party anyone has ever been to? Twenty years from now, you won't forget it!

You could throw a prom in an apartment, in a barn, or in the backyard. Prom could take place on a beach, on a cul-de-sac, on a bridge, or in the middle of a field.

I'm telling you, there's nothing like seeing a sea of people doing the Dougie! There's also nothing like being goosed by a fifty-two-year-old woman in a wheelchair either. (Not that I have firsthand experience with that or anything.)

Wherever and whenever you throw the party, what you will learn is this: what we love is never more important than who we love.

God loved Mephibosheth. (For those of you looking to give your son a unique name, it's an option.) Mephibosheth ate his meals at a king's table. And not just any king, but King David. Because his feet didn't work, someone carried Mephibosheth to King David's table every day.

When I close my eyes, I can see it . . . I can see a man scooping Mephibosheth off the sidewalk and carrying him into the palace, past the group of men that had taunted and teased him every day on the playground as boys. And I can see Mephibosheth sitting next to King David as David tells those gathered around the table what it was like to see Goliath hit the ground.

What would happen if all of us put an extra chair at our dinner table each night and invited someone like Mephibosheth to join us? My parents did it for all kinds of overlooked people. The homeless and the hitchhiker broke bread with us. And so did more refugees than I can count. My parents opened up their home to Vietnamese refugees after the war ended. I cannot remember a time in my childhood when my parents weren't helping someone escape the horrors of war-torn Vietnam.

And of all the refugees who found peace at our dining room table, I think everyone in my family would agree that one of our favorites was Cuc. Cuc has polio. When Cuc walked the streets of Saigon, people would pinch her and yell at her because they believed she had done something evil in a previous life to offend an ancestor. They believed her reincarnated life was punishment for it.

For months, every time Cuc would eat with us, her friends shamed her. They would lift her pant leg revealing a stunted leg, and they would shake their heads in disgust at her. My mom put a stop to that. My mom only stands five feet two inches off the ground, but she is a spiritual giant.

My mom explained to Cuc that she is a child of God. My mom introduced Cuc to Jesus, who healed legs like the one Cuc's friends made fun of. And someday Jesus will throw a party for people like Cuc and my mom.

I'm looking forward to seeing Jesus dance with Cuc.

————————

By most accounts, every great athlete will tell you that the Ironman Triathlon in Hawaii is the most grueling sporting event on the planet. Competitors swim 2.4 miles, ride a bike 112 miles, then wrap the day up with a short 26.2-mile marathon run.

A few years back, the cameramen covering the event for NBC struggled with their assignment. During most Ironman competitions they would focus all their attention on those athletes who were leading the pack. But during this one, they found themselves captivated by another participant who was nowhere near the front of the race.

A father in his forties was pushing, carrying, and pulling his quadriplegic son through the entire race. He swam the 2.4 miles with his son in a special vest being towed behind him. He picked up his son out of the water and put him in a special basket attached to the front of his bike, and he pedaled 112 miles up and down mountainous terrain, leaning, straining, standing, sitting—assuming any posture that might help him bear the load of his son. He then set his son in a carriage and stood behind him, running with every ounce of energy left in his body, pushing him twenty-six miles.

The television cameras were faced with an unusual dilemma—panning to the contestants who were leading the race and vying for first place, or cutting farther back in the race where a father and son seemed to be chasing some other kind of victory. Darkness overtook the day as most contestants finished the race and settled into their hotel rooms to replenish their bodies. But the crowd didn't thin. The crowd grew.

As the sun went down, people showed up. People stood anxiously at the finish line wondering if the father and son would even finish the race, when all of a sudden, someone yelled out, "Here they come!"

Floodlights clicked on down the final stretch of pavement as everyone watched Dick Hoyt, in a full stride, running toward the finish line with his son, Rick. And you should've seen the expression on Rick's face! Jubilant, eyes wide and wild with an excitement his legs and arms could not express.

Rick knew he crossed the finish line because someone loved him enough to help him get where he couldn't get on his own. As for Dick, a look of determination suggested he would not have had it any other way. Exhaustion and all, fatigue and all, perspiration and all—it was all worth it.

Dick Hoyt sleeps well because he lives well. Don't you want to live well too?

The quality of your life is tied to the quality of the love you give to others. God has placed many people around you who need to be exposed to a higher quality of love.

If you want to see a Jesus Prom before you start a Jesus Prom, I invite you to our dance in Lexington. There is no better way to spend an evening. I promise, you will sleep well after you dance the night away. Plan on smiling a lot. Plan on crying a lot. Plan on dancing a lot.

Plan on meeting Jesus and experiencing what heaven will be like.

All you need to know are the hand motions to "Y.M.C.A." And maybe the Macarena.

And all you need to bring is a big heart. You'll get more love than you give away. Way more!

And you'll see why *who* we love is always more important than *what* we love.

NINE

# give (v.)

I canceled Christmas.

Or at least that's what I was accused of.

Several years ago, Christmas fell on a Sunday, and I challenged our church family to spend Christmas visiting and giving gifts to people they normally wouldn't. Instead of coming to church that Sunday, I challenged them to *be* the church that Sunday. Jesus came to us in person. So what better way to capture the incarnation than to go to people in person?

I didn't feel like I was canceling Christmas. I felt like I was promoting Christmas.

The week before Christmas, an eight-year-old Jesus follower in our church, Jacob, went door-to-door in his neighborhood making himself available to do odd jobs. He took all the money he earned and all the money he had saved in his piggy bank, then went to the mall to buy the nicest winter coat he could find.

The reason?

His buddy at school stood shivering in an old, oversize sweatshirt on the playground during recess because his parents couldn't afford to buy him a coat. So on Christmas morning, Jacob handed his buddy a North Face coat and said, "Jesus wants me to give this to you!" It had cost him 160 dollars. He then generously reached into his pocket and pulled out 37 dollars. "This is all the money I have left, and I want you to use it to buy whatever your family needs," he said.

"The only thing that counts," according to Galatians 5:6, "is faith expressing itself through love."

Julie, a six-year-old girl, baked brownies and stood at the entrance to the library at the University of Kentucky on Christmas morning. She gave a free brownie to any college student who walked by.

One Muslim student stopped and said, "Why are you giving away free brownies to total strangers?"

Julie is sassy. So she put her hand on her hip, and in a no-duh kind of tone said, "Because Jesus wants me to. That's why!"

Little did she know that this Muslim student had been wrestling with what he believed, and had been questioning the tenets of his faith for more than two years. Dumbfounded by her emphatic response, he said, "Can I come to church with you?"

"Sure you can!" she blurted out, before consulting her parents.

But here's my favorite part—instead of bringing this PhD student into the big room with the adults, she took him into her children's ministry environment where he sat on the floor and heard a lesson about Jesus' love for Zacchaeus.

After months of sitting and listening, he took a stand for Jesus and was baptized. His family told him they would kill him if they ever saw him. As scary as that threat sounds, he's safe. He's safe because he's saved. And all of it happened because a little girl partnered with Betty Crocker and the Holy Spirit.

Galatians 5:6 says, "The only thing that counts is faith expressing itself through love."

I challenged our church family to go to every restaurant in town on Christmas and buy as many meals for strangers as possible and leave as many big tips as possible. One high school student had gone to the bank and emptied his savings account. He had been saving for a car. He went to the Waffle House, and as he got to know his waitress, he felt like God was saying, "She needs help."

He ordered a seventy-five-cent cup of hot chocolate, then put a thousand dollars in an envelope. He stuck the envelope between the salt and pepper shakers, went outside, and hid in the bushes to watch her reaction. When she opened it, she put her hand over her face and started to cry. Overcome by emotion, she sat down in the booth as he ran back inside and hugged her.

He learned that she was a single mom trying to raise two teenagers by working three jobs. She and her children are now part of our church family, and someday you'll get to meet them because a high school student decided, "The only thing that counts is faith expressing itself through love."

Fifteen minutes later at the same Waffle House, another family from our church walked in and ordered breakfast. Their waiter was a struggling college student who was behind on his bills and had just been told that he would not be able to return the following semester until he paid off his debt. To make matters worse, his car had broken down, and he couldn't afford to pay for the repairs, which meant he couldn't get to and from work.

The family wrote him a check and a note that said, "We believe in you and want you to be able to pursue your dream of being an artist, so this should cover your debt and the next two years of college. We've also enclosed the keys to our car . . . it's the blue Volvo sitting next to the newspaper stand outside. Jesus gave His life up for us, so it seems the least we can do is give you our car."

And they walked home that day!

Like the Muslim student, like the struggling single mom, that young waiter didn't need much convincing to give his life to Jesus because he had already met Jesus in that family.

Galatians 5:6 says, "The only thing that counts is faith expressing itself through love."

I recently applied for a job at the Waffle House in hopes that someone would give me a blue Volvo!

———————

First John 3 says, "If anyone has material possessions and sees his brother in need but has no pity on him, how can the love of God be in him? Dear children, let us not love with words or tongue but with actions and in truth" (vv. 17–18).

We have a generosity yardstick at Southland that says this: "Generosity is not measured by how much we give away. Generosity is measured by how much we keep for ourselves."

Jesus was reclining at a table with friends when Mary anointed His feet with a pint of pure nard. Nard is taken from a plant extract that grows in the Himalayan Mountains. In Jesus' day a pint of it cost a year's wages.

Mary broke the family heirloom open and poured a year's wages on the feet of Jesus. The disciples became indignant and red-faced, and yelled, "Why this waste? This perfume could have been sold at a high price and the money given to the poor" (Matt. 26:8–9).

Jesus looked at them and said, "The poor you will always have with you, but you will not always have me" (Matt. 26:11).

How we would treat Jesus is how we should treat the poor.

I live with the most giving people on the planet. People who birthed a clinic that provides free medical care to three thousand uninsured people in our city. People who feed three thousand hungry people every day. People who have given five hundred homeless men and women a free place to live and jobs to restore their dignity. People who rebuilt an entire Indonesian city after a tsunami wiped it off the map.

If there is a basin of water and a towel and two dirty feet to wash, I know fourteen thousand people who will fight for the privilege of washing those feet. If there were a pint of nard in Lexington, we would not have a problem "wasting" it on the poor.

————————

I had a lawn mowing business as a kid. I made six dollars each time I mowed one person's yard. One summer I mowed fourteen yards each week. I made eighty-four dollars a week and put all my hard-earned dollars in a shoe box under my bed. From time to time I would pull out that shoe box and dump those dollars on my bed to count them—*one, two, three, four, five*. You can buy a lot of baseball cards and Mountain Dew with eighty-four dollars!

For every ten dollars I made, my dad challenged me to give one dollar away. Every week I gave away eight dollars and forty cents.

At the age of eleven I took a homeless man to McDonald's and bought him something warm to eat. His name was Kevin. My dad drove. But I paid.

I learned that Kevin's wife had died in a house fire three years after they were married. Kevin blamed himself. I learned that Kevin needed more than food. He needed someone to listen to him. Listening may be the greatest form of love. People need us to listen to them. I learned how to listen that day. I learned how to love that day.

That summer I bought baseball cleats for a boy named Chico whose dad was in prison. I bought a pillow for a woman named Helen in a nursing home. I bought school supplies for a Vietnamese refugee named Hien.

I also bought three tickets to the movie *E.T.* for my buddies Clint, Jesse, and Tim. My dad drove. I paid.

But what I received was far greater than what I gave, and mowing yards took on a greater purpose. I learned that giving is better than getting. I also learned that names matter. Kevin, Chico, Helen, and Hien . . . as well as Clint, Jesse, and Tim.

Names matter because people matter.

My dad's name was Roy. His shoe box and his heart were much bigger than mine. He was the most generous man I have ever known. He taught me the value of one life. He taught me the value of one dollar—four quarters. Ten dimes—one hundred pennies.

I was watching CNBC one evening, and the host and a panel of economists were discussing the value of the American dollar. They were bemoaning the fact that the

American dollar was depreciating. I'm not an economist, nor do I make or have a lot of dollars. So I'm sure on many levels the host and panelists were probably right.

But . . .

I think the American dollar still has value.

My kids have a piggy bank full of pennies. They love to dump the pennies on the floor and count them. Stacks of Abraham Lincolns. One hundred Abraham Lincolns equals one George Washington. Historians might disagree with that but bankers won't.

How do I teach my kids the value of one dollar?

One billion people live on less than one dollar a day.

I can't sleep because of that reality . . .

CNN reported from Somalia tonight, where five hundred thousand children are expected to die of acute starvation in the next two months. Every five minutes the United States spends six and a half million dollars to pay down the interest on the more than sixteen trillion dollars we owe. We spend three hundred and ninety million dollars a day on interest payments alone.

Giving is better than spending.

Could anyone benefit from less spending and more giving?

I believe everyone could benefit from less spending and more giving.

When I lived in Haiti, I caught a man eating three-day-old macaroni out of my garbage. Thinking I would report him to the police for stealing, he begged me for forgiveness. Both of us started to cry. His tears were tears of desperation. My tears were tears of devastation. I begged him for forgiveness. I decided that day to spend less and give more.

One child dies from starvation every five seconds. In the five minutes it took me to type this section, sixty children died.

Let's give more so more can live.

I am not a mathematician. My wife keeps our checkbook balanced. She also keeps me balanced. That said, I do understand the power of addition. One, by itself, is not a large number. But add one to any other number, and the number grows. If one person asks me to help them and I give them one dollar, that dollar does not have the potential to change that one person's life.

But what if ten people each gave one dollar to one person in need? Or what if one hundred people each gave one dollar to one person in need? Or what if one hundred thousand people each gave one dollar to one person in need?

Change is possible. The potential for change is greater with *we* than *me*.

I work with many people in need. I have many friends who want to help people in need. So we started a Dollar Club. Bad name. Good idea. We meet every weekend. And every weekend everyone gives one dollar to help one person in need. No money spent to give money away. No committees. No hidden fees. No administrative costs. No fine print. No extra charges. No hoops to jump through. No bureaucracy. No government. No red tape. No middleman.

You give a dollar; someone gets a dollar.

We give fourteen thousand one-dollar bills; someone gets fourteen thousand one-dollar bills. Giving has gone up in a down economy.

These are the economics of love.

You will never miss the dollar you give away. Never. Ever.

You will miss the opportunity to change a person's life.

It's change for a dollar.

As a follower among followers, I invite people to bring heaven to earth. And heaven is synonymous with hope. Everyone I know needs hope. The poorest people on the planet are the people without hope. When we bring heaven to earth, we bring hope to people. When we bring hope to people, we end poverty.

Hope is the reason one dollar can change the world. What could happen if you and your friends started a Dollar Club? Pick a better name if you like.

It's easy. Any gathering of friends can do it: a choir, a senior class, a bowling league, a motorcycle gang, your office, your family, your neighborhood, your team. The guys you play golf with, the women you play bunko with, the friends you vacation with—everyone giving one dollar for one person who cannot afford to eat, cannot afford a pair of glasses, cannot afford a winter coat, cannot afford school supplies, cannot afford their prescription medicine, cannot afford their electric bill.

And what about our bigger gatherings?

From basketball arenas to football stadiums. From U2 concerts to Wimbledon. From graduations to bingo halls. From dorms to barracks. From art festivals to marathons. From Apple to Nike. From conversations Bill Gates has with Warren Buffet. From country churches to city churches. From the United Nations to the halls of Congress. One hundred senators equals one hundred dollars. Give one hundred dollars a week to a coach or a teacher in the inner city, and they can multiply it like the fish and the bread.

What if every day, every week, every month, every year, everyone who could give a dollar gave a dollar? Who knows? Maybe a jar filled with one-dollar bills sitting in every government building will convict elected officials to spend less than they bring in. Who knows? Maybe a balanced budget will lead to a balanced perspective.

Heaven on earth. Hope on earth.

It's a perspective.

———————

Hannah's husband committed suicide. He left her with three children and thousands of dollars of debt. He blamed his death on her. Hannah worked two jobs for ten years to pay off the debt, but before she could make the final payment to the bank, she learned she was going to die if she didn't have surgery to repair her heart. Hannah did not have health insurance. Hannah did not have the fourteen thousand dollars needed to pay for the surgery.

Once again, Hannah's heart was broken. Someone told me about Hannah's need, and I shared her need with our church. I did not know Hannah. I still do not know Hannah. I invited everyone in our church to give one dollar. We took fourteen thousand dollars and gave it to the doctor who could repair her heart. I called Hannah to let her know. Hannah cried, but her heart is healing. That is change for a dollar.

When I think about all the problems in our world and all the people who have no hope, it keeps me up at night. It bothers me in a profound way. But then I'm reminded that God doesn't sleep so we can. And from time to time, maybe it's God who keeps me up at night. Maybe God wants me to think about what He thinks about in the middle of the night.

Maybe there is a reason God doesn't sleep.

Maybe that reason is people—people in need.

Frank needed a new roof, so our Dollar Club helped. Julie needed a new wheelchair, so our Dollar Club helped. Jim needed new glasses. Susan needed a reliable car. Valerie needed counseling. The Thompsons needed groceries. The Bateses had funeral expenses. The Vances were evicted.

My dad once told me: "If it's worth anything, it will cost something."

Jesus proved that.

The Bible says, "Though he was rich, for our sake Jesus became poor" (2 Cor. 8:9).

One dollar is a small cost. What could I do with a dollar? What could we do with dollars?

Change the world? Change a city? Change a neighborhood? Change a person?

Change us?

When I give, I get. When I give, others get.

I'm giving more than a dollar. I'm giving love.

Love changes everything.

So give love, because: "The only thing that counts is faith expressing itself through love."

# TEN

# go (v.)

When I was in college, I used to travel on the weekends and preach in country churches that couldn't afford to pay for a full-time preacher. One weekend I drove to a small town in central Kansas. I walked in the front door and was immediately greeted by a middle-aged woman who smiled and said, "May I help you?"

"Yes, ma'am, my name is Jon Weece, and I'm here to preach this morning," I said with a smile. But as soon as I said, "I'm here to preach this morning," she shot me the dirtiest, most sour look you've ever seen, turned around and stomped off huffing and puffing.

I stood there for a few moments trying to figure out what I had done to offend her when another woman walked up and said, "May I help you?"

*That's a loaded question in this church!* I thought. So I took a risk and repeated myself. "Yes, ma'am, my name is Jon Weece, and I'm here to preach this morning."

Once again, as soon as I said, "I'm here to preach this morning," she did the famous crane pose from *The Karate Kid*! (Not really, but she did resemble an all-star wrestler.)

After five awkward seconds of fearing for my life, she took a deep breath, shook her head, and said, "I'm sorry. I don't want to take it out on you. Our church just went through an ugly split and the other *half* of our church is meeting in a house down the road. They have a huge sign out front, so you can't miss it."

Well, I felt terrible. I apologized to her in one sentence and thanked her in the next. I drove down the only street in town, and sure enough I found the other *half* of the church. There was a huge refrigerator box in the front yard, and on the box someone had spray-painted the word *CHURCH*.

I pulled in the driveway, got out of my car, and a man in his late seventies stood in the doorway staring at me. Instead of opening the door, he looked me up and down through the glass, then cracked the door as if frightened by the sight of me and said, "Are you the boy they sent to preach?" and then pulled the door shut again.

"No, sir," I wanted to answer. "I was just driving through the middle of Kansas and it was the quality of your sign and the hospitality of everyone around here that made me want to stop in and spend a morning with you!"

Of course I didn't say it. Instead I said, "Yes, sir. I'm the boy they sent to preach."

He let me in his house and led me to his living room where I discovered the other half of the church. There were *four* people seated on a floral-print couch that sagged in the middle. One of the arms of the couch was held together with duct tape, and one of the cushions looked like a T. rex had gotten hold of it.

Before I could introduce myself to the other *half* of the church, the old man who let me in the house barked, "Why don't you lead us in a time of singing?" (I will affectionately refer to that man as the "Church Nazi" from here forward.)

I'm not much of a singer, but due to the size of the audience and the fact that I thought I might be on *Candid Camera*, I decided, why not? So I asked if they had any favorites they wanted to sing, and the four people decided on three songs.

I started to sing, and halfway through the first verse of the first song I noticed none of them were singing. Instead they were staring at me with mortified looks on their faces, as if I had just shot their favorite pets. I ended up singing three specials for the four people on the couch. The whole time I kept thinking, *My friends are going to pop up from behind the couch and shout, "Ha! We got you!"*

That was wishful thinking.

Meanwhile, the Church Nazi had dozed off in his recliner and was actually snoring. When he finally stirred, he said, "It's time to collect the offering," and handed me a bag. In my home church someone always prayed before the offering was collected, so that's what I did. When I tried to pass the bag to the Church Nazi, he wouldn't take it. Instead he looked at me like I was the village idiot and said, "We always sing the Doxology before the offering."

I knew what he meant by, "*We* always sing . . ."

So I sang the Doxology for them!

I passed the bag to my amigo in the La-Z-Boy, and he passed it from the recliner to the couch. When it came back to me, no one had put any money in it. Not a dime! Whatever they were spending their money on, it wasn't furniture or joy.

It was time for me to preach. I had a standard thirty-minute message that I cut back to twelve minutes. I was tossing illustrations and paragraphs on the fly. By the time I was done preaching, everyone had fallen asleep with the exception of one sweet, elderly woman in the middle of the sagging couch. She had been encouraging and affirming the entire time I preached, and since she was the only person in the room still conscious, I wanted to leave a good impression with her.

I stuck out my hand to thank her, and she folded her arms, puckered her lips, and squinted at me in response. She was mad. And I could tell I was the person who had made her mad. She pointed her finger at me and said, "Son, we always sing a hymn of invitation."

I scratched my head and thought, *For whom? Rip Van Winkle over there? The squirrels outside? Who is going to come to Christ in this place?*

But then again, I decided, why fight it now? So I sang all four verses of "Just As I Am." And of course, no one came forward to accept Christ.

I drove back to the college I was attending, and I remember sitting in the parking lot outside my dorm wishing I could get the last four hours of my life back.

When we stop moving, we start dying.

Too many churches are filled with too many people who are *fans* of Jesus but not *followers* of Jesus. The body of Christ doesn't need more spectators. The body of Christ needs more servants; it needs more people who will go.

"Servants can go places kings can't," my friend Gary says. He is right.

Jesus commanded us to "go and make disciples of all nations" (Matt. 28:19). Jesus wants us to make more and better disciples. Jesus wants us to help everyone everywhere become a follower. And the way we help everyone everywhere become a follower of Jesus is by serving everyone everywhere in the name of Jesus.

One-third of the world's population claims to follow Jesus. That means two-thirds of the world's population doesn't claim to follow Jesus. We need to serve those four billion people in the name of Jesus. We can't wait for them to come to us. We have to go to them.

My friends Ted and Bev run an orphanage in Taiwan. For forty years they've rocked babies to sleep, changed their diapers, and placed them in loving homes. Ted and Bev are servants who help people see Jesus.

Charlie spent his Saturdays changing the oil for single moms with cars. Along with some friends with pickup trucks, he started delivering furniture to people in need. Now they provide food and clothing and other material items to fifteen thousand families a year in their hometown. When you meet Charlie, he'll tell you, "I'm just a redneck from Whitley County!" Charlie is a servant who helps people see Jesus.

Myron teaches graduate-level courses to pastors throughout Europe. Brent plants churches in cities that don't have churches. Rachel meets medical needs among the poorest people on earth. Brian throws parties that connect students on a major university campus to God and one another. Karen counsels children with emotional challenges. Max helps homeless men find jobs. Steve and Andrea buy pieces of garage-sale furniture, fix them up, and give them to families in need. Craig trains business leaders in closed countries.

All these people are my friends. All these people are missionaries. All these people decided to go where people in need live. None of them wait for people to come to them. They are servants who help people see Jesus. They go places kings can't go and often do things kings wouldn't do.

In the city where I live, there is an antique store that used to be a church building. What was once filled with people is now filled with dusty relics. Every year in our country seven thousand churches will close their doors. Most of them close because they quit going to people in need. Most of them close because they quit serving people in need.

When we stop moving, we start dying.

The church was never meant to be confined or defined by four walls. The church was designed to be a mobile, agile, flexible, and tangible movement of the Spirit of God. Wherever Christians go, that's where the church is. We don't *go* to church. We *are* the church.

Every day the church goes into classrooms. Every day the church meets in doctors' offices. Every day the church gathers in restaurants. Every day the church hangs out in factories and at construction sites. Wherever you go, that's where the church is. In the second century when a massive plague swept through Roman cities, everyone left for fear of being infected. As everyone ran out, Christians ran in to care for the sick and dying.

The church needs to be in the worst neighborhoods and in the worst schools and in the worst cities in our world. When everyone leaves, we move in. We roll up our sleeves and serve in such a way that the worst places on earth become the best places on earth. Our mission is to bring heaven to earth so we can take earth to heaven.

———————

My friend Shelly is a dental hygienist by trade. She moved to Haiti to serve children in need. Her heart is bigger than the

island. Late one night as Shelly walked home from a Bible
study, she was jumped from behind, thrown to the ground,
and attacked by a man she didn't know. As he attempted to
remove her clothing, she managed to fight him off and run
for help. With her shoulder dislocated, she pushed open the
first door on the first house she came to and collapsed on
the floor in shock.

An elderly woman by the name of Granka came to her
aid. Granka and Shelly became friends because of that
traumatic experience. And in the months that followed,
Shelly didn't feel sorry for herself or become bitter toward
the Haitian people. Instead, Shelly served Granka in the
most beautiful and humble ways. And the love of Jesus
in Shelly helped Granka fall in love with Jesus. Watching
Shelly baptize Granka in the ocean is forever etched in my
memory.

And yet that memory pales in comparison to the Sunday
that Shelly walked into church with Parnell, the young man
who had attacked her. Shelly was walking to church when
she passed him on the road. He had just been released
from prison, and though Shelly's mind raced with fear, she
knew she had come to Haiti to love people like Parnell.
Shelly knew that forgiveness is most powerful when it is
least deserved and least expected. With fear in her voice
and love in her heart, she invited him to join her.

There was an audible gasp when they walked in together.
And for months they continued to walk into church
together. Each week Shelly sat next to her assailant on the
front row and helped him navigate the invitation of God

to a new life. Parnell and Granka will both be in heaven because Shelly decided to go where people in need of heaven live.

After years of mapping the continent of Africa, Scottish explorer and missionary David Livingstone died among the people he served. Before shipping his body back to his family in Britain, they removed Livingstone's heart and buried it in the soil of Africa. His body is in one place, but his heart is in another.

Wherever you go, give your heart to the people there. I left part of my heart in Haiti. I plan on leaving the rest of it in Kentucky. I want to bury my heart in the hearts of the people I serve.

My friend Jani is giving her heart to women who feel trapped in the exotic dance industry. Along with hundreds of women in our church, she helps women find hope and healing. I love it when people do more than wear their hearts on their sleeves. I love it when people give their hearts away.

What keeps most of us from giving our hearts away is fear.

When my son, Silas, was two years old, he sprinted down the hallway in the middle of the night saying in a panicked voice, "To infinity and beyond! To infinity and beyond!"

When I scooped him up, I realized he was dead asleep and was having a bad dream. Bob the Builder was obviously beating up Buzz Lightyear!

When my daughter, Ava, was three years old, she wouldn't go to bed one evening, so I picked her up and asked her why. Her bottom lip came out and tears gathered in her big brown eyes. She said, "Can I sleep with you and Mommy tonight if the big red chicken comes to my room?"

"Tell me about the big red chicken," I said, trying not to laugh.

"Every night he pokes his head out of my closet door and then flies around and around my room," she said in a very animated way.

I turned to Allison and said, "I think someone has put LSD in our daughter's Cheerios."

As followers of Jesus, we face our fears with faith. Going to certain places to serve certain people will require a lot of faith. Whatever requires the most faith is what you need to do. Faith pleases God and helps us grow. The more faith we have, the less fear we have.

I bet Shadrach, Meshach, and Abednego kept their garments in a hall closet, and when company came over for dinner, they pulled them off the hangers and passed them around the table saying, "You can't smell smoke, can you?"

I bet David had his sling mounted above the fireplace in his palace with a simple inscription that said: I picked up five rocks, but God only needed one.

I bet Abraham kept his knife in a shoe box under his bed, and each year on Isaac's birthday, he pulled it out and ran his fingers over the blade.

I bet Mary kept her maternity clothes, Peter kept the sandals he wore when he walked on water, Noah kept his olive branch, Lazarus kept his grave clothes, and Paul stared at the scar from his snakebite.

What do you have to show for trusting God? What do you have to show for obeying Him? What fear have you overcome with faith?

We go wherever God wants us to go; do whatever God wants us to do and whenever He wants us to do it.

———————

My best friend in Haiti was a young man named Sove. He was the handyman at the school where I taught, and he taught me the language of the Haitian people even though he couldn't read or write. He treated me like a brother. For years Sove was skeptical of my faith. For years I never tried to force my faith on him.

Years into our friendship, Sove was diagnosed with AIDS. I went to visit him in a hospital where more people die than survive. He was in a large room filled with men. Words on a page cannot describe the smells, the sights, and the sounds of the suffering that took place in that room. Sove's once healthy and muscular frame was wasting away. He couldn't have weighed a hundred pounds— literally skin on bone.

I knelt down beside his mat, and before I could get a word out, he started to cry. Knowing that his hang-up with God was human suffering, I braced for the worst and prayed for the best. Through tears, Sove said, "I'm afraid to die, and I don't want to be."

I cried for my friend.

"Tell me more about Jesus," he said. "I want to know more about Jesus."

I stopped crying and shared that Jesus had come to bring heaven to earth.

Sove pointed to a young man lying next to him. Naked and covered in sores, the young man's tongue was swollen to the size of his mouth, making it difficult for him to talk. I leaned in close and said, "I don't know what you have done for my friend, but thank you."

"Jon," Sove said, "he prayed all night and sang all night. I want what he has."

One dying man telling another dying man where to find life.

I cried again. If Sove was the only person to follow Jesus because of my time in Haiti, I would go again. People need what you have, and what you have is life. God put life in

your heart. Open your heart up and give that life away.
Give your heart away.

The people who need Jesus the most won't come to you.
You have to go to them.

Always remember, Jesus did the same for you. He came to
you so you could go to Him.

So go.

## ELEVEN

# suffer (v.)

Several years ago I was in a department store with my family doing some last-minute Christmas shopping. My son, Silas, who was four years old at the time, said, "Dad, I really need to go to the bathroom." Emphasis on the word *really*. I had no idea where the bathroom was located, so I asked a clerk, who graciously pointed me in the right direction. The tricky part was that Silas and I had to walk through the lingerie section to get there.

I walked with my head down—doing my best not to make eye contact with anyone or anything in the area—when out of the blue Silas shouted, "Dad, look!" Now that's a dangerous thing to say in the lingerie section. Before I could stop him, he dashed and darted through the racks of unmentionables to a table where he grabbed a bra and started jumping up and down.

"Dad," he said, "on *Tom and Jerry* they use this as a parachute!"

If that wasn't enough, he climbed atop the display and put it to the test. Bra above his head, he jumped.

Naturally, all the women in the area laughed!

It's always funny when it's not your kid.

As I scooped him up in my arms, I heard a lady behind me say, "Hey, aren't you the preacher at Southland Christian Church?"

I spun around and said, "No, ma'am. I work at the local prison, and this little guy is one of our escaped convicts!"

In the first century, wherever the followers of Jesus went, everyone would ask, "Hey, aren't you . . . ?" And when they answered, "Yes, I am . . ." what followed was more than humiliation. What followed was persecution. The pain that followed Jesus' followers also followed Jesus to the cross. Suffering was the language of the early church. They were fluent in it. It became their native tongue.

Kevin Carter won a Pulitzer Prize for a picture he snapped in southern Sudan. In the foreground of the photograph is a little girl who is starving to death. In the background of the photograph is a vulture. In her weakened and emaciated state, the little girl is unable to stand. Her head is buried in her hands. Her knees have buckled beneath her naked frame. She is minutes away from death. And the vulture waits and watches.

Three months after he took the picture, Kevin Carter took his own life. There was something about seeing a little girl sit down and a vulture stand up that seemed out of balance to him—a global disequilibrium, a global sloping of the floor that is more than the earth tilting on its axis. There is a gravitational pull to suffering that pulls us down.

It's difficult to stand up when you're suffering. It's easier to sit down.

———————

My mother-in-law, Betty, lived with us for three years while she battled cancer. Before she died, Betty would sit at the dining room table for what felt like hours at a time. She couldn't muster the strength to lift her head off the table long enough to drink a protein shake. The chemotherapy and radiation sapped her of all her strength. Physically and emotionally she was weak. It was hard to watch her sit and suffer.

Betty's story reminds me of another brave woman. We don't know her name. What we do know is that she was suffering and had been suffering for twelve years. That's a long time. She wasn't battling cancer or MS or cystic fibrosis or Alzheimer's. The Bible says she couldn't stop bleeding. "She had suffered a great deal under the care of many doctors and had spent all she had, yet instead of getting better she grew worse" (Mark 5:26).

Her bleeding created more than a medical problem. It was a major social problem too. She was barred from worshiping in the temple. Under Mosaic law, her condition—like leprosy—limited her social interaction with people for fear that someone might touch her and become unclean.

My mother-in-law suffered with family and friends around her. This woman suffered alone.

When I was a little boy, my parents started taking in Vietnamese refugees. I don't remember a time when people from other countries weren't living with us. The first family had a daughter named Hau who had been so traumatized by the sights and sounds of war that every time a commercial airliner flew over our backyard, she would run to a tree, sit down, put her fingers in her ears, and cry. Tears would stream down her face, and she would stare off into space for a long time—catatonic—never saying a word.

When we suffer, we want to sit down. When we suffer alone, we want to sit down and shut up. Words are hard to come by when we suffer.

Back to the story of the suffering woman. As Jesus walked through her town, a large crowd pressing against Him, He passed her. I don't know if she was in the middle of the crowd or on the outskirts of the crowd. What seems clear is she wasn't standing up. She was sitting down. And she didn't say anything to Jesus. Instead she quietly reached out and touched the edge of His garment. "Immediately her bleeding stopped and she felt in her body that she was freed from her suffering" (Mark 5:29).

When her bleeding stopped, Jesus stopped too. He wanted to know who had touched Him. His disciples laughed because everyone was touching Him. But Jesus knew someone had touched Him because power had left His body and gone into someone else's.

Suffering does that. Suffering drains people of power. That's why it's easier to sit than stand when we suffer. When we suffer, dignity leaks out of us. When we suffer, hope leaks out of us. Suffering siphons life out of us.

Jesus came to suffer *with* and to suffer *for* people. That's why Jesus was called the Suffering Servant. Jesus poured Himself into people who had been emptied by suffering. And if we claim to follow Jesus, we will follow Him into crowds of suffering people and pour the life and love that was poured into us into them.

If we claim to follow Jesus, we will help sitting people stand back up. We will speak up for those who have shut up. And there are many people who are sitting down and not speaking up for many reasons.

Legend has it that Ernest Hemingway once wrote a story that was so short it only had six words. Some have said it was Hemingway's greatest work because it was his most personal work. He wrote: "For sale—baby shoes, never worn." Maybe you've experienced the pain of burying a child. It will knock you down and knock the wind out of you.

I performed the wedding ceremony for two of my friends, James and Lauren. Nineteen days later I spoke at Lauren's funeral. Married and buried in nineteen days. Maybe you've experienced the pain of burying a spouse. It will knock you down and knock the wind out of you.

I know people who say, "The more faith you have, the less you will suffer." That's not been my experience, nor the experience of my friends who have faith. And it definitely wasn't my Savior's experience.

Sometimes the more faith you have, the more you suffer.

———————

My mom taught me a song when I was a little boy that had a line, "Oh be careful little eyes what you see, for the Father up above is looking down in love." Twenty years ago I experienced the lowest point I've ever reached in my life because my eyes were only focused on myself.

I was nineteen years old, I was living in Haiti, and I had just finished my second prizefight with malaria. It won, and I lost. I lost a lot of sleep and a lot of weight. I also lost a lot of perspective. Emotionally, physically, and spiritually, I found the bottom of the barrel.

When I was on the brink of giving up and moving back to the states, a Haitian pastor invited a few close friends and me to preach in his home church in the mountains. I knew I needed to accept the invitation, so I did.

After a day's hike into a remote area of northwest Haiti, we arrived at a makeshift church building on Friday evening. It had a roof but no walls, and hundreds of people sat on rocks and hard benches while others stood in the back and to the sides. They sang for a few hours, and one testimony after another was given about the goodness of God. Following a time of prayer, I was invited to preach. We were already three hours into the church service, so I kept the message short.

After the people sang some more, the pastor invited me to preach again. My first sermon wasn't deserving of an encore, but I preached a second time. After the service ended, we were led to a baked-mud, thatched-roof hut where we would sleep for the weekend. As each of us rolled out our bedding, I took my shirt off and started spraying down with mosquito repellent. The owner of the hut walked in carrying an oil lamp for us to use, and when he saw me dousing myself, he laughed.

That happens a lot when I take my shirt off in public places.

"You won't need that tonight," he said, setting the lamp down on a small table. "We don't have mosquitoes this time of year."

I smiled. Having just suffered the effects of a mosquito-borne disease, I was glad to know I might get my first good night's sleep in a long time. As he walked out of his hut, I heard my host say, "We don't have mosquitoes. We have rats."

"Please tell me they make such a thing as Deep Woods Rat Repellent!" I said to my buddies.

We turned off our flashlights to go to bed. As soon as we did, we heard what sounded like someone smashing a bag of Ruffles potato chips above our heads. We quickly turned our flashlights back on, only to be greeted by dozens of eyes.

Yep. Rats. Everywhere.

They came out of the thatched roof and scurried around us and on us, using us like we were interstate highways. I began to call down fire from heaven. Imprecatory prayers poured out of my mouth: "Dear God, even though I walk through the valley of the shadow of death, I do not want You to prepare a table before me in the presence of mine enemies! Oh Lord, strike these rodents down and burn them up with Your eternal flamethrower! In Jesus' name, amen."

If you don't believe in hell, you need to visit that hut.

Needless to say, we didn't wake up the next morning because we never really went to sleep the night before. We spent the entire day teaching on the life of Jesus. When dinnertime rolled around, we were tired and hungry and they fed us parts of a goat that God never intended man to eat. When we finished the meal, to wash it down they served us water that was a different shade of clear than I was familiar with.

We preached again that night, and when it came time to go back in the hut, I told my friends, "I'm sleeping outside." So I lay down on a hillside with my clothes on, and within ten minutes of falling asleep, it started to rain.

God has a funny sense of humor.

Back inside the hut, I spent another sleepless night with the rats.

Sunday morning rolled around, and my buddies and I were deliriously tired. We preached on the crucifixion and resurrection of Jesus, and anytime you preach on that subject, people respond. A handful of men and women surrendered their lives to Jesus and wanted to be baptized. As I stood on top of the mountain looking for water, an older woman smiled at me, pointed, and said, "There is water over there."

I looked "over there" and I didn't see the water. All I saw "over there" were more mountains. We walked up one hill and down another hill. For hours we walked and walked and walked until we finally arrived at the water.

The water had animals in it. The water had people bathing and doing laundry in it. The water was green and thick. The English vocabulary doesn't have words to describe how bad it smelled. But the people from the church didn't seem to care. They slipped off their shoes and stepped in without any hesitation.

And that's when I heard it, thousands of miles away from the city and church where I was raised. It was as if my mom was standing in the water behind me singing, "Oh be careful little eyes what you see . . . Oh be careful little eyes what you see . . ."

In the midst of my pity party, I had lost sight of Jesus. But I found Him again on the faces of people. As we baptized them, their smiles told me they weren't concerned about the parasites in the water. They weren't put out by having to walk miles to be baptized. They didn't care if their church building didn't have soft seating.

My new brothers and sisters in Christ helped me see Jesus. They helped me realize the blood that dripped from the four corners of the cross must find its way to the four corners of the earth. Because suffering doesn't discriminate. Suffering permeates every people group on earth. No one is safe from suffering. And Jesus came to suffer with and to suffer for people. Jesus came to end the suffering on this earth.

One of my favorite lines in the Bible is, "And God will wipe away every tear from their eyes" (Rev. 7:17). Someday God will wring the earth dry of every drop of sweat, every drop of blood, and every teardrop. That day is coming. Until that day comes, can I invite you to suffer with and to suffer for people? Can I invite you to stand up and speak up for people who are sitting down and people who have shut up?

Will you help stop the bleeding?

———————

I ride the city buses in Lexington once a month. I get on and get off at different bus stops each time. It helps me meet different people with different problems. A lot of the people who ride city buses are suffering alone. Sitting on buses with them has helped me see why they struggle to stand up.

Vince is a war veteran. His wounds are visible and invisible, physical and emotional. Vince invited me to his apartment to see some of his war memorabilia. As Vince and I got off the bus, he hobbled down the sidewalk and up the flight of stairs to his second-story apartment. What was easy for me was difficult for him. By the time we sat down at the kitchen table, he was winded and wincing in pain. He didn't talk for a while because he couldn't.

I was reminded that my freedom isn't free. My freedom cost Vince the lower part of his leg and a big part of his heart. Vince showed me a few albums filled with pictures of his army buddies, a medal he won for bravery, a letter he received from the Pentagon, and another letter from a senator. Vince was once a popular athlete and a college-bound student. What once was, isn't what is. Today Vince lives alone. Today Vince spends most of his time sitting in silence.

"Loneliness is the leprosy of the modern world," said Mother Teresa.

Vince doesn't need money from me. Vince doesn't need me to feel sorry for him. Vince needs my time and my attention. Giving my time and my attention to Vince doesn't feel like suffering. It feels like sharing.

Paul said, "Share each other's troubles and problems" (Gal. 6:2 TLB).

When we share each other's suffering—your problem becomes my problem, and my problem becomes your problem—we help each other stand back up. When we share each other's suffering, we lighten each other's loads.

I was watching an ESPN documentary a few years ago about two high school wrestlers in Cleveland, Ohio. At the age of eleven, Leroy Sutton was walking home from school when he slipped in some loose gravel and fell on a train track. His backpack somehow managed to get stuck to one of the rails, and he was unable to get free and escape an oncoming train. That day, Leroy Sutton lost both legs; one was amputated just below the knee and the other just above the knee.

Dartanyon Crockett grew up without parents to care for him. Every day he fended for himself, and there were times when he lived on the streets for days without food to eat. Dartanyon was born with Leber's disease, an eye condition that keeps him from seeing anything farther away than a few inches. He is legally blind.

Little did Leroy or Dartanyon know their paths would cross in an inner-city high school; little did either of them know they would come to rely on each other to get through life. Dartanyon carries Leroy wherever Leroy needs to go—all 170 pounds of him—while Leroy helps Dartanyon know where to go. Dartanyon provides strength and Leroy provides vision. Together the two of them are able to navigate the ups and downs of life.

We need each other. And there is someone who needs you to sit with them in the waiting room, or at the funeral home, or on the bus so they can stand back up.

Who is that person?

Don't let them get lost in the crowd.

Don't let them suffer alone.

TWELVE

# remember (v.)

The Vietnam Veterans Memorial in Washington DC is striking for its simplicity.

Etched in a black stone wall are the names of 58,286 Americans who died in the Vietnam War. Since its opening in 1982, that stark monument has stirred deep emotions.

Some visitors walk its length slowly, almost reverently without pause. Others stop before certain names, remembering their son or fiancé or fellow soldier, wiping away tears, tracing the names with their fingers.

For two Vietnam veterans—Robert Bedker and Willard D. Craig—a visit to the memorial must be especially poignant, for they can walk up to the long ebony wall and find their own names carved in the stone.

Because of a clerical error, both of them were incorrectly listed as killed in action; they were thought to be dead, when really, they are alive.

In my mind I make the journey up the hill to Golgotha every day. It's a war memorial I need to visit. I don't want to forget the cross. Rembrandt painted a picture of the cross. At first glance, his rendering is really no different than most Renaissance paintings—a hill, three crosses, a dark sky, and a crowd. What separates Rembrandt's painting from other depictions of the crucifixion is a man who stands in the crowd dressed in seventeenth-century clothing. He stands out from the other observers.

Rembrandt knew enough to paint himself into the picture of the cross.

I don't want to forget the cross.

So I run my hand over the contours of the wood. And with each return visit I find my name etched in the bloodstained grain. And I remember: I was once dead, but now I am alive.

My wife called me on my way home from work and said, "I just want to prepare you."

"Prepare me for what?" I asked.

"Your son"—I love when she says that, as if Silas isn't her son too—"spray-painted a big orange *X* on the driveway. And by big, I mean *big*!" she said.

In his defense, the day before we had drawn pictures on the driveway using chalk. Also in his defense, I'm the one who'd left out the can of spray paint. I pulled onto our street, and I could already see it from a hundred yards away. It was like what you would paint on a freeway if you were trying to help a helicopter make an emergency landing!

*X* marks the spot.

When I walked in the house, Silas stood behind his mom. Shame. Fear. All the things that make me want to hide made him want to hide. I grabbed him and hugged him and said, "Hey, *X* is my favorite letter in the alphabet! If I were going to spray-paint a letter on a driveway, I would have chosen an *X* too!"

As long as I live, I'll never forget this—he reached in the front pocket of his camouflaged pants and pulled out a wad of wrinkled-up one-dollar bills that he had been saving to buy a paintball gun. He handed the money to me and started to cry. As quickly as he gave it to me, I gave it right back to him.

"Silas, I got this one!" I said as I hugged him. "This one's on me. Why don't we go to Lowe's? I bet they have something that can remove a spray-paint stain from concrete."

We went to Lowe's and bought a chemical product and a hundred pieces of steel wool, and I spent the next four hours on my hands and knees in thirty-degree weather scrubbing concrete.

My brother Jud came to visit a few weeks later. Silas took his uncle by the hand, walked him out to the driveway, and said, "Look, this is where I painted the driveway! And look, it's not there anymore!"

"Did you clean it off?" my brother asked.

"No, I wasn't strong enough to make the stain go away. But my dad was," Silas answered with pride.

God does what Silas did. God turns stains into stories.

My friend Greg was stained by alcoholism. God scrubbed the stain away.

My friend Lisa was stained by prostitution. God scrubbed the stain away.

My friend Todd was stained by pornography. God scrubbed the stain away.

God is strong.

Don't forget that. Remember that.

In 1995 I climbed in a car with some friends from college, and we drove to the site of the Oklahoma City bombing. We parked our car several blocks away, and I remember how quiet it was as we walked toward the epicenter of the blast. The FBI had put up a chain-link fence around the federal building that had been destroyed, and it had become a sort of memorial for the victims.

I walked slowly, almost cautiously, around the block, reading the different tributes. People had left bundles of flowers and stuffed animals and pictures of loved ones.

And toward one end of the fence, a dad who had lost his little boy had paper-clipped a picture of his son to the corner of a poster board. With a black magic marker he had drawn a rudimentary cross. And under the cross he had written these words: "Because of the cross I can forgive Timothy McVeigh. Because of heaven I'll see my son again someday."

Sin puts an X on our hearts. Sin holds us hostage to the stain. But God forgets our sin. We need to remember that God forgets. Don't forget that God forgets. He doesn't see the stain. He sees the story. In His eyes, your story is not marked by sin. In His eyes, your story is marked by grace.

Remember that. Don't ever forget that.

———————

One of Satan's greatest weapons against us is his timing. He not only knows what to say and to whom to say it; he knows when to say it. He likes to whisper lies to you when you are hungry, tired, lonely, and far from God. The voice of Satan was deafening in the Garden of Gethsemane. And I find it ironic that the ugliness of the cross began in the beauty of a garden. Jesus was pleading with the Father to come up with a Plan B, an alternative to the cross.

Three times Jesus begged His Father for an escape route, and three times the answer that echoed back from heaven was *no*. And how did Jesus respond to the response of the Father? He sweat drops of blood. I don't like to remember that, but I need to remember that. The medical term for sweating blood is *hematidrosis*: when the capillaries in the forehead burst due to stress and the blood mixes with sweat and flows out of the pores in the skin.

Jesus said, "My soul is overwhelmed with sorrow to the point of death" (Matt. 26:38). That is a sadness I do not know. That is a pressure I have not experienced. Jesus was beaten with fists and sticks, was flogged, was spit on, had a crown of thorns driven into His scalp, and had nails driven between His wrists and ankles.

I am a sinful man. I am a very sinful man. I do not deserve to have another man die for me.

When I was in the second grade, I got on the school bus and walked to the seat where my brother and I always sat together after school. The bus would stop at my school first, then go to the junior high and pick up Jud. Between the time I got on and the bus picked up my brother, a sixth grader and a few of his cronies decided to pick on me.

They started with words, then moved to flicking me in the ear, and eventually ended with punching me really hard on the head and shoving me against the window. By the time we stopped at the junior high, I was trying to hide it, but I had shed a few tears. When my brother Jud got on, he knew something was up. He sat down and put his arm around me. I remember the look of concern on his face.

"What happened, Jon?" he asked.

At first I didn't want to tell him, because I didn't want to seem weak. But a funny thing happened. All the other elementary kids on the bus who had been picked on by the same bullies turned around and said, "Those guys hit Jon!" Even if I wasn't going to say anything, they all knew my older brother could do something about it.

Jud turned to me and asked, "Is that true? Did they pick on you?"

All I did was nod my head.

"Jon, I want you to stay here no matter what happens."

I watched my brother push up the sleeves of his shirt and take a deep breath. Anytime my brother rolled his tongue up in his mouth, he meant business. This wasn't our first rodeo, and it definitely wasn't our last. Jud stood and walked straight to the back of the bus. Three boys jumped up to meet him, scared out of their minds. The odds didn't matter. My older brother channeled his inner Mike Tyson and whooped all three of them!

When the bus driver finally pulled my brother off and walked him down the aisle toward the front of the bus, everyone on the bus erupted with cheers. It was as if a hero had come home from war. The bus driver sat my brother down in the front seat and told him not to move. From my seat, I watched Jud rub his busted lip. Then he looked at me (his hair all messed up), smiled, and gave me a thumbs-up as if to say, *No one messes with my kid brother!*

Jesus got tired of the bully messing with people He loved. Jesus got tired of sickness and death and all that Satan and sin had brought into this beautiful world. And that's why Jesus took it on the chin for us. That's why Jesus took a stand for us on a cross.

Jesus, our older brother, is tired of Satan bullying us—and I'm telling you, He's big enough and strong enough to do something about it. Friends, there's a day coming when Jesus will push back His sleeves and face Lucifer once and for all.

And it won't be a fair fight.

The reason it won't be a fair fight is because Jesus didn't stay on the cross. Jesus didn't stay dead. He rose from the dead.

Death lost.

Life won.

And there is an empty tomb to prove it. We need to remember that every day. Every day we need to be reminded that cemeteries are temporary resting places. There will be no funerals, no obituaries, and no tombstones in heaven.

United Nations officials did an inspection of the morgue in the city where I lived in Haiti. As they were passing through the facility, one of them saw movement near a pile of dead bodies. It would have been enough to make the hair on anyone's neck stand up. An older man had been brought to the morgue to die. His family could no longer care for him, so they put him where he would eventually end up.

Jesus rescued us from certain death. Jesus pulled us out of the pile. And on Sunday we gather with other people who were found in the morgue so we can paint ourselves into the picture of the cross. We read and we sing and we pray and we feast in preparation for the wedding celebration we've been invited to. Church on Sunday is the dress rehearsal, yet so many people have gotten in the habit of skipping it.

"I love Jesus but hate the church," they say.

If someone said, "Jon, I love you, but I hate your bride, Allison," I would have a problem with that person. Allison and I are one and the same.

Jesus and His bride, the church, are inseparable. Anyone who says they hate the church hates the man who died on the cross *for* the church. Jesus didn't just die to save people. Jesus died to save *a* people. The church is His family. He is our brother, and His dad is our dad! And in the same way that I need Jesus, I need you and you need me. We are inseparable.

———

I like to climb mountains with my brothers. We don't say a lot on the way up because there isn't enough air to breathe. But once we get to the summit, we're speechless for a different reason. Have you ever been in the presence of pure beauty? Have you ever seen something so pristine and so untainted by the sin of this world that words escape you?

Standing on top of the world, my brother Joe managed to quote Psalm 121:1: "I lift up my eyes to the hills—where does my help come from? My help comes from the LORD, the Maker of heaven and earth."

And that's all he needed to say—maybe all he could say. Standing within reach of the ceiling of earth, there was something so satisfying about being so small. There was something so satisfying about being still and silent.

Each Sunday I climb a hill to a cross with my eternal family, and we stand in the presence of pure beauty. On the peak of Calvary's hill, we find strength for our weakness, grace for our sin, healing for our wounds, and life for our death.

Together we always remember, so we never forget.

## THIRTEEN

# receive (v.)

Grace requires this verb.

Years ago we lived across the street from a boy named Jared. He was our neighborhood's version of Dennis the Menace. When I came home from work, he would be standing on my front porch, excited to show me the different bugs and small creatures he had caught in the creek behind his house.

One day I pulled in the driveway, and Jared was jumping up and down with joy, smiling from ear to ear. He was shirtless and shoeless and covered from head to toe in mud. His left hand was bandaged from a bike accident, but in his right hand he was holding a three-foot-long blacksnake.

That poor snake. Jared had a death grip on it and flung it around like a bullwhip.

"I had to crawl through a drainage pipe to get him. He bit me once," he said, "but it was worth it, Mr. Weece!"

When Jared learned that we were moving to a different neighborhood, he showed up on packing day with his hands behind his back. Based on past history, I had reason to be alarmed about what he might be hiding.

"I've got a surprise for you," he said with a slow Kentucky drawl.

"Is it venomous?" I joked.

"No sir, we don't have any venomous snakes in this part of the state." He then filled me in on the different kinds of nonpoisonous snakes that live in central Kentucky and the Amazon rainforest. After a five-minute herpetology lecture, it was as if he suddenly remembered why he had come to see me; and without any setup, he revealed his gift. With cupped hands he offered me a porcelain doll that had obviously been dropped and superglued back together again.

"We cleaned out my sister's room last weekend, and I was going to shoot at this with my slingshot," he said. "But I thought you might like something to remember me by, so I'm giving it to you instead."

"Are you sure you didn't already shoot it with your slingshot?" I asked. The head of the doll had been glued back facing the wrong direction.

"No, I dropped it on my way over here, so I had to use my mom's glue to fix it up," he said with obvious pride in his handiwork. Then, as though he were getting ready to tell me where Jimmy Hoffa was buried, he looked around and whispered, "Please don't tell my mom I used her glue. She gets madder than a hornet when I use it without asking."

"Your secret is safe with me," I said. And I thanked him for the gift.

I'm not good at receiving gifts. When I was a kid, my two older brothers wrapped up a refrigerator box and put it next to the Christmas tree with my name on it. In the weeks leading up to Christmas, the anticipation of what was inside nearly killed me. When I opened it, it was full of packing peanuts and a poster of Rambo.

Don't get me wrong. I loved Rambo as much as the next red-blooded American kid. But when you think there's a bike or a dog in the refrigerator box and all you get is a poster . . . that borders on cruel and unusual punishment.

Though I wish I could blame my problems on Sylvester Stallone, the real reason I struggle to receive gifts is because of pride. I don't want to owe anyone anything. Of course, the truth is that I owe God more than I can pay back.

I can't afford grace.

And what I love about God is He doesn't demand that I pay Him back for it. When it comes to grace, I don't need a monthly payment plan.

All God asks of us is that we receive His grace. And inside the gift of grace are two gifts we get to unwrap and enjoy: justification and sanctification. Justification and sanctification are sometimes referred to as the double cure of salvation.

Look at this verse with me: "By one sacrifice he has made perfect forever those who are being made holy" (Heb. 10:14).

What God has declared us to be—made perfect forever (that's justification), God helps us become—being made holy (that's sanctification). He saved us (justification) and will keep saving us (sanctification) until we are safe with Him. What makes grace a profoundly beautiful gift is that God has done (justifying) and is doing (sanctifying) something for us that we can't do for ourselves. And He does not demand anything in return.

We don't earn it. We don't work for it. And most importantly, we don't deserve it.

We receive it.

Grace.

How do we respond to such a gift?

With gratitude. With humility. With joy.

I spoke at the funeral of a young woman who was murdered by her boyfriend. As heartbreaking as the details surrounding her final moments on earth were, nothing broke my heart more than learning of her estranged relationship with her dad. They'd had a falling-out over money, and he had kicked her out of the house and told her he never wanted to see her again. Despite repeated efforts on her part to reconnect with her dad, he would hang up whenever she called and tear up any letter she mailed.

He refused to forgive her.

After everyone else left the graveside, he just sat on the front row as a cold winter wind blew through the tent and over his daughter's casket. Standing just a few feet away, I noticed a small tear streaming down his cheek, refusing to stay hidden under the dark sunglasses that projected a macho demeanor. What started as a raindrop soon became a roaring river of tears.

He sobbed.

Alone.

"I never got a chance to tell her I loved her," he said over and over again. "I never got a chance to say good-bye to my little girl."

As I put my daughter to bed that night, I was reminded of David's words: "[God] does not treat us as our sins deserve" (Ps. 103:10).

When I reach out to my Father, He doesn't turn me away; rather, He receives me. Though I deserve to be kicked out of my Father's house and disowned because of my prodigal ways, Luke 15 tells me that I have a Father who will run to me, embrace me, and celebrate my return. I don't deserve such treatment—but I am grateful for it, humbled by it, and filled with joy because of it.

The more love I receive from the Father, the more love I want to give to the Father. Jesus said, "If you love me, obey me" (John 14:15 TLB).

Obedience may be the most appropriate response to the grace of God. If God went to the extreme of dying on a cross to save us, He obviously has our best interests in mind. And if God has our best interests in mind, we can trust that what He asks us to do is in our best interests.

Some of us struggle to obey God because we had an earthly father who demanded obedience without love. A lot of dads demand obedience and their reason is, "Because I said so!" God invites us to obey, but His reason is, "Because I love you."

Whether you had the worst dad or the best dad, God is not like your dad. He's better. He's always better.

————————

Silas was four years old when, while we were in the drive-thru at McDonald's, he told me he was going to throw up. I didn't have anything to hand him, so in a moment of panic I took off my shirt and gave it to him. I hadn't considered what I would look like when I pulled up to the window to pay.

There I sat in my Honda Accord, window rolled down, wearing sunglasses but no shirt. I know it may be difficult

RECEIVE (V.) | 161

to tell from the picture on the back of the book, but I'm no Abercrombie model. The teenage girl working that day handed me my Coke. Then after an awkward pause, she smiled and said, "Hey, I know you!"

"No you don't," I quickly said.

"You're the preacher at Southland!" she said with the excitement of a cheerleader. And if that wasn't humiliating enough, she followed it up with, "You baptized me!"

It's a good thing they don't offer refunds on baptisms. After seeing me with my shirt off, she might have wanted one.

God endured far more humiliation in His effort to clean me up from the sickness of my sin. God has given me more love than anyone else in my life ever has or ever will. I don't want to be a spiritual hoarder. When God says, "Look after orphans and widows in their distress" (James 1:27), I do it because I've received so much from God that I can't possibly keep it to myself.

God's love is too big, and my heart is too small to contain it all.

"God loves a cheerful giver" (2 Cor. 9:7).

Notice what it doesn't say—"God loves a reluctant giver or a guilt-ridden giver or a scared giver." Our motivation to give is joy. We receive so much love that we have a lot of love to give away.

Would the people around you describe you as a generous person? Would the people around you describe your church as being a generous people? Grace will change your church the way it changed you. What's missing in some churches isn't better music or better preaching or a better location.

What's missing in some churches is grace.

Jesus told the church in Ephesus, "You have forsaken the love you had at first" (Rev. 2:4).

I haven't been to Ephesus, but I've been to a church like that. I don't have a problem if stingy and rigid and mean people want to get together on Sundays. I just wish they wouldn't identify themselves as a church.

Like truth, the church is not a *what* but a *who*. Like truth, the church is Jesus. And when a church doesn't have grace, it doesn't have Jesus. A church without Jesus isn't a church—it's a building. Our world doesn't need more buildings. We need more churches. We need more grace.

We need more Jesus.

A high school student who was turned away by a local church because of the way he was dressed on Sunday wrote a poem entitled, "Jesus Hates Me." He passed it out at school the next day.

> *Jesus loves me this I know, for the Bible tells me so. Little ones to him belong, they are weak, but he is strong.*

*Preach to us what to believe, give us disease and
poverty.*
*Demand our praise, say you're our friend, tell us how
we live in sin.*
*Feed us lies and teach us greed.*
*Those with their own minds are scorned,*
*Exile those who don't conform.*
*Thank you Lord for what you've given—violence,
racism, and hate.*
*Our children murdered and our women raped.*
*And they ask why I have no faith?*
*Jesus hates me this I know and the ones who are
not clones.*
*Little ones who don't belong,*
*He is weak, but I am strong.*

———————

Nothing breaks my heart more than people who have received grace but refuse to give grace to others. At each of our campuses we have a wall that people sign when they receive the grace of Jesus. Some people call it the Name Wall. I call it the Lamb's Book of Life. It's my favorite part of each building because each name represents a story.

Ken was married four times and was violently abusive to his first three wives. It was his fourth wife who helped him see his need for Jesus. Ken received grace. Ken signed the wall.

Rebecca was raped and had an abortion. The shame she felt kept her from running to God and His people. Instead she ran into the arms of dysfunctional men. A woman named Fannie loved her and helped her see the need for Jesus. Rebecca received grace. Rebecca signed the wall.

After one of our weekend services, I prayed with an exotic dancer who said, "My whole life I've wanted a dad, and you're telling me that God wants to be my dad. It sounds too good to be true!"

"It is good and it's true. He wants to be your dad, and He wants you to be His daughter," I told her.

"As I am?" she asked.

"As you are," I said.

She received grace. She signed the wall.

From addicts to prisoners to homeless men and women, it's more than a wall. It's a snapshot of grace. It's a glimpse of heaven.

Grace doesn't exclude. Grace includes.

In 2009 I preached at a big church in a big city on our need to love the poor as Jesus commanded. My closing illustration was about an AIDS patient in Africa and Bono's statement that some people in this world are "victims of latitude."

Afterward I was confronted by a man who wanted to know why I was so passionate about "helping people halfway around the world." He viewed AIDS as God's punishment for sexual immorality and believed "those people got what they deserved." He held a Bible and wore a necklace with a cross on it.

"Jesus didn't just die for me. Jesus died for everyone," I said.

"We will have to agree to disagree," he snapped back.

"I don't know that we can agree to disagree about grace," I said as I fought back tears.

# FOURTEEN

# verbatim (adv.)

My grandma spent the majority of her twenties and thirties living on empty.

After a few failed marriages and a few tragedies in her life, she believed God could never love her, forgive her, or fill her with life again. She felt as if she was wearing a scarlet letter anytime she stepped foot in a church building. Like Macbeth, she thought she had a stain that she couldn't hide; a stain that everybody could see.

It wasn't until one Sunday morning when she heard a sermon on the love of Jesus that she understood how she could be saved by grace and how she was designed to live by grace.

The preacher visited with her and my grandpa and invited them to come back that night for another service. They thanked the preacher for the invitation, but told him they probably wouldn't come back.

For some reason my grandma decided to get out their best clothes that afternoon and iron them, just in case they changed their minds. My grandparents didn't have "church clothes." All they owned were "dancing clothes." My grandparents loved going to local halls and bars to dance. So she pressed her dress and his pants and polished their dancing shoes.

About the time she finished, my grandpa walked in the bedroom and said, "What do you say about going to church tonight and hearing that man again?"

Hearing her husband say that, a man who had never shown an interest in church or God, my grandma knew God was nudging them. The preacher preached another message on grace that night, and my grandma remembered, "It was like he had read my mail and had eavesdropped on my conversations. I wanted so badly to go forward and be saved." But after the service, they got in their car and drove off without responding.

They drove down the street to a local diner and ate dinner. Halfway through the meal, my grandpa looked at my grandma with tears in his eyes and said, "What do you say we go down to the river and watch some baptisms?"

My grandma smiled and cried at the same time. As they approached the banks of the river, a leader in the church told my grandma and grandpa they might want to change out of their nice clothes because the river was so muddy.

"I can't think of a better way to start my new life with Jesus than by dancing into that river and right out of it!" my grandma told the man.

She died three years ago, but my grandma is still dancing today. After ninety years of dancing here on earth, she is now dancing in the presence of her Father.

The church my grandma served for fifty-three years is a small country church in Eldon, Missouri. Besides being known for the best chili cheese hot dog in the world, it's a rather nondescript community in the middle of the heartland. You wouldn't be drawn to the church for its location or building. You would be drawn to the church because of its people.

After my grandma's funeral the people of the church cooked a big country meal for our family. The food was so good that if churches had couches, I would have curled up and taken a nap that afternoon after eating. I'm convinced the cooks in heaven will know a thing or two about Southern cooking and comfort food.

You know God isn't afraid of a little butter!

Ninth Street Christian Church loves Jesus, and it shows. They understand their role as the body of Christ on earth. They understand the purpose of the church is to be an identical twin to its founder.

"Be imitators of God, therefore, as dearly loved children," Paul said, "and live a life of love, just as Christ loved us and gave himself up for us" (Eph. 5:1–2).

The goal of the church is to become increasingly more like Jesus. Jesus loved people, which means the church should love people. If Jesus did it, we imitate it.

Verbatim.

Two of my least favorite phrases are *kind of* and *sort of*. The word *verbatim* carries connotations of exactness and precision. We don't *kind of* love people. We don't *sort of* love people. We love people the way Jesus loves us. We are mirrors of His sacrificial love, impersonating His every move.

If imitation is the greatest form of flattery, Jesus should be flattered by the actions of the church.

Christians frequently visit Southland and say, "I'm new to town and am church shopping. What can you offer me?" Wouldn't it be great instead if people came to church and said, "Here's what I can offer the church"?

Southland is trying not to be a consumer-driven church. We're not selling a product. There are plenty of churches in America that cater to their shoppers. And what I've noticed is, consumerism fuels entitlement. And entitlement fuels a mind-set that says the customer is always right.

A simple reminder: we own nothing and manage everything.

Our time, talents, and treasures are not ours. It's all God's. My life was bought at a high price. I am owned. What is mine is really His. The church is not mine and it's not yours.

The church is His. It's all about Jesus, and it will always be all about Jesus.

When you get some time, read the last book of the Bible. It's called Revelation because of who it reveals. Revelation reveals Jesus as He was, as He is, and as He will be. In chapter one, Jesus is a High Priest. In chapter five, Jesus is a Slain Lamb. In chapter nineteen, Jesus is a Conquering King.

I want to know Jesus as He was, as He is, and as He will be. The more I know Jesus, the more I will be able to live like Him—verbatim.

If Allison and I ever have twins, our son, Silas, wants us to name one of them Jesus Weece and the other Disco Weece.

That's problematic on a lot of levels.

My brother wanted to name one of his sons Buck. Buck Weece. His wife wasn't as big of a fan of the *Little Rascals* as he was, so they went with Jake and Jared instead.

I have friends who are identical twin brothers. They attended different colleges. One went to college in Missouri. The other went to college in Kansas. And from time to time they switched places with each other. Those of us who were close to them never knew. They took each other's tests, wrote each other's papers, and even dated each other's girlfriends.

That's problematic on a lot of levels.

But there's nothing problematic about becoming more like Jesus, whether individually or collectively. A Christian is the singular representation of Jesus on earth. And a church is the plural representation of Jesus on earth. Those of us who are close to Jesus should struggle to see any difference between a Christian and a church.

My prayer in writing this book is that it would be our individual goal and collective goal to be like Jesus.

Verb-atim.

# add-verbs

Don't just serve. Don't just give. Don't just love.

Serve joyfully. Give sacrificially. Love recklessly.

It's amazing what can happen to your life when you add adverbs. Adverbs add so much to verbs.

Adverbs such as radically, outrageously, spontaneously, abundantly, frequently, honestly, differently, beautifully, secretly, courageously, and generously.

It's amazing what *ly* can do to the quality of your life.

When I read *how* the people of the Bible lived, the word *faithfully* comes to mind.

When I look at *how* most people today are living their lives, the word *pathetically* comes to mind.

It's a choice. *How* you live is a choice. So *how* are you going to live?

Sadly? Boringly? Indecisively? Reluctantly? Fearfully?

If you live like that, you are not really living.

*How* we live will determine *how* people see Jesus. So let me end where I started.

Jump.

And don't just jump.

Add an adverb.

If it were up to me, I would tell you to . . .

. . . jump quickly.

# acknowledgments

Alli—I love you. Thanks for loving me back.

Ava & Silas—Your love helps me see God.

Mom—Your love is selfless.

Julie, Joe, and Jud—Your love let me tag along.

B and Kelly Frye—Your love is generous.

Chris Hahn—Your love frees me up.

The staff and elders at Southland—Your love is patient and humble and fearless.

The Southland family—Your love is simple, yet deep.

Mike Breaux—Your love believed in a 26-year-old kid.

Wayne Smith—Your love is evident every Saturday night.

Kyle Idleman—Your love is lifelong friendship.

Don Gates—Your love is in the details.

The Thomas Nelson team—Your love took a risk.

Brian Hampton, Joel Miller, and Chad Cannon—Your love is partnership.

Kim Pascual—Your love made this book happen.

Scott Alexander and Carmen Niehaus—Your love shared more than Twizzlers.

Paul Williams—Your love gave me perspective and rest.

Gary Black—Your love allowed me to dream big at Burger King.

Dale Thomas and Jim Cox—Your love is protective.

Dan Hamel—Your love is insight.

Evan Mossbarger and Craig Avery—Your love is courageous.

Gordon Walls—Your love never gives up.

Cam Huxford, Dave Stone, Jeff Stone, and Tim Harlow—Your love is encouragement.

Chad Johnson and Mark Hostetler—Your love is like a brother's.

Mary Helen Bosch—Your love is intercession.

Chris Love, Kato Hall, and Todd Justice—Your love has my back.

Stephen Dawahare—Your love is supportive.

Jay Johnson—Your love gets me around.

Bob Goff and Don Miller—Your love challenged me to put my heart on paper.

Max Lucado—Your love helped me overcome shyness.

Jakina Stark—Your love challenged me to write.

Mark Scott, Mark Moore, JK Jones, Kenny Boles, and Matt Proctor—Your love showed me Jesus.

Janene MacIvor—Your love poured over every word.

Mallory Perkins and Kristen Vasgaard—Your love will be held and highlighted by many.

Mark Weising, Mike Seaton, TJ Rathbun, Jay Irwin, and Chad Seeber—Your love put in some long, creative hours.

Justin Meeker, Derrick Purvis, Brendan Harriff, and Noah Jacobus—Your love is in the code and font.

Katy Boatman, Emily Lineberger, Kristin Cole, and the rest of the team at A. Larry Ross—Your love provides humble promotion.

Dixon Kinser—Your love is in the meat of the curriculum.

The Lodge Family—Your love filled my empty cup.

# about the author

Jon is married to Allison, and they have two children, Ava and Silas. For the past fourteen years he has been the Lead Follower at Southland Christian Church—a community of fourteen thousand Jesus followers in central Kentucky who love people in extravagant ways. Prior to moving to Lexington, Jon lived in Haiti for four years.

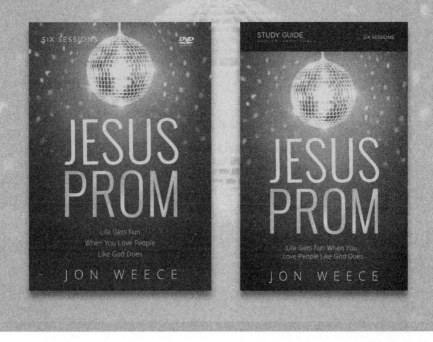

Nouns need verbs. That's more than just a grammatical truth—it is a spiritual truth. The noun *Christian* and the noun *church* require action verbs to fulfill their purpose. That's why Jesus invites Christians and churches everywhere to perform the greatest action of all: *loving people*.

In this curriculum, Jon Weece paints a picture of the verbs that Jesus loved. You'll meet people like Deanna, who was in the porn industry before she met the *love* of Christ; and Rebecca, who saw what the church could *be* and adopted eight children with physical and mental challenges. You'll meet Bill, a former drug dealer who *saw* God change his life; Stephen, a businessman who understands the power of *giving*; and Dewayne, a man who struggles with his past but *remembers* that Jesus has set him free. You will also meet Brewster, who started a unique *dance* for 2,500 physically and mentally challenged adults—a dance called Jesus Prom.

*Jesus Prom* is an extravagant party that celebrates the very people Jesus died to love. By the end of it, you'll want to join the dance!

**For videos, sample chapters, and all
*Jesus Prom* news, please visit JesusProm.com.**